Praise for Aron Ain and

WORK INSPIRED

Kronos is a consistent and powerful growth engine. Now we learn its secret: putting people first, both because it's the right thing to do and because it's the path to long-term success. I deeply admire Aron Ain's philosophy, and others will, too.

—DEVAL PATRICK, Managing Director, Bain Capital,
and former Governor of Massachusetts

Employees want to work for companies that cherish values such as family, ethics, hard work, and philanthropy. When they find these organizations, employees feel inspired to deliver high levels of performance. Aron Ain takes you on a tour of a values-based corporate culture that you can develop within your own organization.

—ROBERT KRAFT, Chairman and CEO,
The Kraft Group

Technology gets all the hype, but in my experience, a focus on people is what consistently distinguishes the best companies from the merely good ones. Aron Ain's book shows why building an authentic company culture is as important to long-term success as any other business decision. It may well be the one from which all great things follow.

—DAVID M. SOLOMON, CEO, Goldman Sachs

Aron Ain's *WorkInspired* is a valuable resource for any leader looking to build an organization rooted in employee engagement and a shared value system.

—STEPHEN A. SCHWARZMAN, Chairman,
CEO, and Cofounder, Blackstone

Many companies claim that "our people are our most valuable assets." But no business leader I know has done more to turn that old cliché into a strategic source for growth than Aron Ain of Kronos. In *WorkInspired*, Aron takes readers step-by-step through principles and practices that have helped Kronos win and grow—mainly by inspiring its own workers to realize their full potential and having each other's backs. Kronos's bottom-line success is proof positive that Ain's commitment to creating a satisfying, challenging—and kind—work environment is a very hard-nosed business strategy indeed. *WorkInspired* shows us all how to execute it.

—ROBERT L. REYNOLDS, President and CEO,
Putnam Investments and Great-West Financial

Aron Ain's *WorkInspired* describes how Kronos has continued to reinvent itself by focusing on culture and mobilizing the power of its people. Ain succeeds in breaking down his approach to a series of powerful policies, programs, and leadership behaviors that many companies have overlooked. Required reading for anyone seeking to build a thriving and sustainable business in the digital economy.

—SHIRA GOODMAN, former CEO, Staples

Kronos has mastered "workforce innovation that works." Here, its inventive and imaginative CEO describes how he created one of the 100 best places to work, and shares the principles that leaders and managers need to create a high-functioning culture built on trust, transparency, collaboration, and innovation.

—DAVID WIPPMAN, President, Hamilton College

WorkInspired is an essential guide for building a winning culture, and it all starts with one person—you! As Aron Ain knows, how managers and leaders treat people day-to-day matters. Ain provides tips and strategies that managers and leaders can put into practice right now, one informal conversation at a time. An enjoyable and compelling read.

—STEVE PAGLIUCA, Cochairman, Bain Capital, and
Managing Partner and Coowner, Boston Celtics

If every manager nurtured their workforce the way Kronos does, the professional world would be a different place. Aron Ain gives his employees the opportunities and tools to succeed using a refreshing and enlightened approach. The result is sky-high employee engagement that attracts young people to Kronos. Read this important book and learn the secrets.

—JACQUELINE MOLONEY, Chancellor,
University of Massachusetts Lowell

Aron Ain is a next-level leader—the kind who gets things done the *right* way by respecting people, giving them a vision to believe in, and creating a culture in which they can excel. In *WorkInspired*, he shares his unique approach with the world. I hope every leader or manager reads this book, and takes its lessons to heart.

—ERIC HOLCOMB, Governor of Indiana

Read this useful book by Aron Ain, who provides the leadership behaviors that create an environment where people love their jobs. Many are amazingly simple, yet many leaders don't do them! After *WorkInspired*, you will.

—CARLOS RODRIGUEZ, President and CEO, ADP

How do you get a large organization to become as innovative and nimble as a startup? Aron Ain's answer is to create ways to help your team succeed and spread a *culture* of innovation across the enterprise. His book delivers nuggets that apply to all managers.

—ERIK WEXLER, CEO, Providence St. Joseph
Health–Southern California

With leadership, two things matter: A clear strategy, and the right culture. Aron Ain delivers on both fronts in this engaging and inspiring book. If you lead people, *WorkInspired* is a compelling blueprint for making this happen.

—STEVE SADOVE, former Chair and CEO, Saks Inc.

There are legions of motivational experts and consultants armed with their latest anecdotes to make the case for an engaged workplace. But rarely do you hear the whole story of what it takes to build and sustain an engaged workplace from the person who did it. With *WorkInspired,* we have a long-tenured CEO letting us have a good look at what it really takes. Aron Ain has truly provided us with a gift . . . a must-read for anyone who wants to tap into the power of their people!

—LEN SCHLESINGER, Baker Foundation Professor, Harvard
Business School, and President Emeritus, Babson College

Kronos serves as a textbook example of how building a great culture builds phenomenal shareholder value. The model and lessons are so compelling that the story warrants a full book, not just a case study. Fortunately, Aron Ain has provided just that—a compelling and useful read for any leader or manager.

—ALEC ELLISON, Founder, Outvest Capital,
and former Vice Chairman, Jefferies

In this highly personal book, Aron Ain presents a refreshing new framework for driving Hall of Fame–level investment results, one that rests first and foremost on the behavior of individual leaders. As Ain compellingly demonstrates, the very personal qualities that make a leader outstanding as a spouse or parent are identical to those required to create and shape a high-trust, high-performance team culture. Ain's book will be an inspiring and essential read for anyone seeking to become a whole-person leader.

—DAVID R. TUNNELL, Partner, Hellman & Friedman

Aron Ain shares a series of lessons on how leading organizations can excel, whether delivering exceptional patient care, producing great products, or delivering outstanding service. We all have a responsibility to create environments where people love to work. Thank you, Aron, for pointing the way.

—KEVIN TABB, CEO, Beth Israel Deaconess Medical Center

Do the best leaders achieve success by genuinely caring about their employees? Aron Ain answers with an exuberant, "Yes!" as he shares the extraordinary story of Kronos to show how to cultivate human capital to ensure your success. I'm happy to give *WorkInspired* my highest recommendation.

—MARSHALL GOLDSMITH, author of the
#1 *New York Times* bestseller *Triggers*

I've become so enamored with Aron Ain and Kronos that I'm constantly telling other business leaders to be more like them. Through *WorkInspired*, Aron has now provided the road map. More happy employees and customers are sure to follow!

—JAY ASH, Secretary of Housing and Economic
Development, State of Massachusetts

Many people know about Kronos and its track record of outstanding business performance. They might not know about the company's deep commitment to the communities that it serves, or its efforts to prepare college students for successful careers. As Aron Ain convincingly argues in *WorkInspired,* serving the community and building a culture that employees feel proud of is like jet fuel for organizations today, leading to a motivated, highly productive workforce and enhanced performance. I strongly encourage managers and leaders everywhere to read this insightful book.

—MARTY MEEHAN, President, University of Massachusetts

Tech companies come and go, but Kronos is still here, bigger and better than ever. Aron Ain's marvelous book, *WorkInspired*, sheds valuable light on the Kronos success story, suggesting how organizations can make themselves sustainable, even in the most dynamic and competitive of markets. Every manager or leader who aspires to greatness will want to read this book and follow its lessons.

—MARK BENJAMIN, CEO, Nuance Communications Inc.

Aron Ain has identified practical advice to help managers motivate employees. If leaders want to learn how to gain a strategic advantage from strong employees, they will find it in *WorkInspired*.

—JOHN PRIOR, CEO, Needham & Company

Ain's playbook for building a high-performing workplace and culture pours forth in this endearing, entertaining narrative. His humble, authentic leadership style should be carefully studied by senior executives as a valuable case study worthy of emulation.

—JEFFREY BUSSGANG, Senior Lecturer, Harvard Business School, and General Partner, Flybridge Capital Partners

Kronos has grown steadily because it empowers its employees, who then deliver world-class products and services to its customers. This valuable book cues us all into the specific practices that truly put customers first.

—RANJAY GULATI, Jaime and Josefina Chua Tiampo Professor of Business Administration, Harvard Business School

Aron Ain has built an organization that innovates while also staying true to its deeply ingrained, humanistic values. His is leadership with heart, and it deserves emulation. I hope employers not only read *WorkInspired* but apply its lessons.

—LAURIE A. LESHIN, President, Worcester Polytechnic Institute

To achieve long-term success, the best-run companies know you need a better people strategy. Kronos has one, and in this eminently useful book, Aron Ain shares it with the world. This book will be a must-read for all leaders—certainly at our portfolio companies. I give it my full recommendation.

—CHINH CHU, former Cochair, Private Equity Group, and former Senior Managing Director, Blackstone

Once in a while, a book like *WorkInspired* arrives with the power to truly transform organizations. Read it, and you'll understand how compassion, family, respect, and service to others are essential to business success.

—RONALD LIEBOWITZ, President, Brandeis University

Aron is a very special leader. Kronos's success is exceptional and very exciting. In a very simple and accessible way, *WorkInspired* presents new approaches to engaging people within your organization. This book is full of practical ways to keep your staff at the center of your performance. This is the kind of reading that definitely inspires me!

—Satya-Christophe Menard, CEO,
Global Education Market, Sodexo

Aron Ain's leadership style is personal and genuine. By sharing this highly successful approach to employee engagement, customer satisfaction, and business success, Aron offers a proven strategy in building an inspired workplace around the globe.

—Chris Anderson, President,
Massachusetts High Technology Council

Aron Ain is an inspiring figure in the technology space, not just because of what he's achieved but how he's achieved it. Likewise, Kronos is living proof that a company can achieve sustained results by living its ideals and making room for *everyone* to contribute. Read Ain's book, and you'll likely become a better manager or leader. You'll also, I suspect, become a better person.

—Mohamad Ali, President and CEO, Carbonite

In today's intense battle for tech talent, Aron Ain provides an authentic people strategy for business success—one that has rocketed his company to the top of the charts as one of the best places to work, while doubling the business to over $1 billion. His book is a must-read for leaders and managers seeking to build their own cultures where people love to work and take pride in driving organizational success. Drawing on his four decades of experience, Aron skillfully weaves in examples to illustrate key principles, providing the reader with the insights and tools they need to "work inspired."

—Tom Hopcroft, President and CEO,
Mass Technology Leadership Council

Aron Ain understands the critical relationship between happy employees and business success. His book lays out how to create environments where people can forge friendships, feel hopeful about the future, and do purposeful work. If you want simple, actionable ideas for how to transform your culture, get *WorkInspired*.

—ANNIE MCKEE, Senior Fellow, Graduate School
of Education, University of Pennsylvania,
and author of *How to Be Happy at Work*

In *WorkInspired*, Aron Ain reveals the secrets to building a company culture that celebrates people, cultivates managers, and creates a positive change. As evidence that Ain's advice is effective, Kronos has been named a Best Place to Work several times over. I always recommend people to work at Kronos, as I recommend people to read this book!

—DAN SCHAWBEL, author of *Back to Human*,
Promote Yourself, and *Me 2.0*

Aron Ain is one of the most thoughtful leaders I've met. He understands that managing people is a privilege, that it takes courage, and that a culture that values management is the key to winning. *WorkInspired* is packed with new ideas from a leader who's mastered the art of motivating employees.

—ADAM BRYANT, creator of the *New York Times* "Corner Office"
series on leadership, and Managing Director, Merryck & Co.

WORK
INSPIRED

WORK INSPIRED

HOW TO BUILD AN ORGANIZATION WHERE EVERYONE LOVES TO WORK

Aron Ain

Mc
Graw
Hill
Education

New York   Chicago   San Francisco   Athens   London   Madrid
Mexico City   Milan   New Delhi   Singapore   Sydney   Toronto

Kronos, the Kronos logo, Workforce Dimensions, Workforce Central, Kronos Workforce Ready, Timekeeper Central are registered trademarks and Workforce Innovation That Works and Kronos Paragon are trademarks of Kronos Incorporated or a related company. All other trademarks, if any, are property of their respective owners.

3 4 5 6 7 8 9   SCI   23 22 21 20 19 18

ISBN   978-1-260-13617-3
MHID   1-260-13617-5

e-ISBN   978-1-260-13618-0
e-MHID   1-260-13618-3

Library of Congress Cataloging-in-Publication Data

Names: Ain, Aron J., author.
Title: WorkInspired : how to build an organization where everyone loves to
    work / Aron J. Ain.
Other titles: Work inspired
Description: New York : McGraw-Hill, [2019]
Identifiers: LCCN 2018027544| ISBN 9781260136173 (alk. paper) | ISBN
    1260136175
Subjects: LCSH: Corporate culture. | Organizational behavior. | Leadership. |
    Job satisfaction.
Classification: LCC HD58.7 .A346 2019 | DDC 658.3/14--dc23 LC record
    available at https://lccn.loc.gov/2018027544

McGraw-Hill Education books are available at special quantity discounts to use as premiums and sales promotions or for use in corporate training programs. To contact a representative, please visit the Contact Us pages at www.mhprofessional.com.

To my wonderful wife, Susan,
my remarkable daughters, Danielle and Hillary,
and to Kronites everywhere,
who inspire me each and every day.

CONTENTS

AUTHOR'S NOTE

To protect the privacy of Kronos employees, I've referred to individuals mentioned in this book by their first name only. Unless noted, all quotes come from personal interviews, internal Kronos correspondence, postings on internal and external Kronos social media pages, and other internal Kronos documents. In crafting this book, I've freely incorporated text from these materials as well as publicly available Kronos documents without quotation or attribution. The result, I hope, will be a text that is clear, accurate, and pleasant to read, and that is also true to my voice and perspective.

INTRODUCTION

I've spent my career working at Kronos˙ Incorporated, the Massachusetts-based, billion-dollar global software firm founded in 1977 by my brother Mark. You might not have heard of us, but chances are we're touching your daily life.

Our initial product was the first microprocessor-based time clock, a device that recorded, totaled, and reported employee hours. Since then, we've continued to build time clocks—we've shipped over 1 million of them and counting. But over the years, as technology and industries have evolved, we've introduced a variety of sophisticated cloud workforce management and human capital management software applications that have shaped the way organizations the world over do business.

Today, under the banner Workforce Innovation That Works™, approximately 5,500 Kronos employees—or "Kronites," as we call ourselves—around the world create, sell, and service software that helps organizations track the time their employees work to ensure that everyone is paid properly; that employees are scheduled based on skills, preferences, seniority, availability, and historic business data; and that organizations are better able to comply with complex labor regulations. Our products also help organizations hire employees, track their performance, run payroll, and perform many other workforce-related tasks. We believe that great businesses are powered by great people, and that to be a great business you need to create and manage an engaged workforce. We build our software for our customers' industries and employees with employee engagement firmly in mind.

Kronos customers include some of the world's largest and most respected brands. All told, more than 35,000 organizations across over 100 countries—including more than half of the Fortune 1000 and thousands of hospitals, universities, and government agencies—use our products to drive better business outcomes in every imaginable industry. More than 40 million people use a Kronos solution every single day!

I'm inspired by what we do—and I've been at it for a while. I joined Kronos in 1979 right out of college, doing everything from selling our time clocks to stopping by the office at 2 a.m. when the security alarm went off. I worked my way up from there, playing leadership roles in nearly every functional group. As my career progressed and I moved into management, I came to develop what I sensed was a fairly unique philosophy, one built around the singular importance of employees. Lots of executives claim to put employees first, but when I became our company's CEO in 2005, I had a chance to put my philosophy to the test.

We had gone public in 1992, opened many offices in the United States, established a presence in countries such as Australia, Canada, Mexico, and the United Kingdom, and achieved $500 million in annual revenues. Behind the scenes, we had done our best to treat people right, offering competitive salaries and benefits to acquire the best talent. By most any standard, we were a really good company. But I thought we had the potential to become even better, and also significantly bigger. I wanted us to grow our revenues to $1 billion and to enter new international markets. I felt that we could achieve such ambitious goals, but we needed to make some big changes. In 2007, we took the company private, a move that I thought would free us to focus on our longer-term vision and would free me up personally to devote more of my time to core parts of our business. In the wake of that move, and as I found my footing as a CEO, I began to concentrate more on our people, treating them according to what I believed them to be: a powerful *strategic weapon*, one that Kronos hadn't yet fully leveraged.

As great as our employees were, we hadn't prioritized the development of our workforce as a key part of our growth strategy. As a result, although our employee engagement scores were above the norm in our industry, we had trouble attracting and retaining the best people. In some parts of our business, our annual employee turnover topped 40 percent. Although people seemed to like working at Kronos and although we had a number of longtime employees, employees didn't *love* Kronos, and they didn't see our organization as a unique and extraordinary place to build a career. That's what we changed—and it's what this book is about.

As a new CEO, I felt that we couldn't continue to create great products or deliver great services without attracting and retaining great people. But that, in turn, would require that we become a better place to work, giving our employees more of what they wanted out of an employer. We needed to revamp and expand our human resources function, which at the time lacked foundational processes and technology, not to mention a strong focus and understanding of best practices. Little by little, we would have to work on our culture, making it more caring, trusting, transparent, collaborative, and innovative.

How would we pull this off? I didn't have all of the answers. In fact, I had very few of them. As a manager and leader, I'd always taken personal satisfaction in creating environments in which people felt motivated to excel. I'd been fortunate enough to be raised by parents who modeled values like caring, honest communication, and trust, so I was inclined as a CEO to build a culture infused with those values. But beyond that, I didn't yet understand what it would take to *institutionalize* a great culture and create an organization that, from top to bottom, was a wonderful place to work. What I had at my disposal was primarily a strong drive to treat people well and get the most out of our workforce. The media often celebrated companies that were "great places to work," but what was so special about those other companies? What did they do that we weren't doing? Why couldn't *we* be one of them?

Our drive to institutionalize a great culture got a boost in 2010 when we hired a seasoned executive with a strong quantitative background as our chief people officer. Many organizations marginalize the human resources function, but soon thereafter we appointed our chief people officer to our executive committee, making it clear that I personally backed what we were doing to create an inspiring and innovative culture. We then took a series of experimental steps to enhance our culture and become a truly unique place to build a career. We did this, to be clear, not because I wanted Kronos to be "nice" to people—which of course I did—but because I was convinced that focusing on people and culture was the soundest possible *business* strategy.

We had been collecting data on employee engagement for some time, but it had largely been a "check the box" kind of exercise. Now we began to work with engagement more intensively. We performed a quantitative and qualitative analysis of the main drivers of engagement, identifying development and innovation as the biggest factors—and after further refinement, we discovered that manager effectiveness and a feeling of connectedness to the company's mission and strategy were also critical. Then we took action around those drivers to better allow us to attract, develop, manage, and retain top talent. We rolled out a slew of new programs, processes, and benefits that our people wanted, branding them so employees around the world understood and valued them. We defined and branded our culture itself, calling it *WorkInspired* and linking it to three core competencies: character, competence, and collaboration. We've since tied these competencies to our business strategy, leadership, performance goals, competency assessments, selection practices, reward and recognition programs, and merit and incentive programs and processes. We called our culture *WorkInspired* because we think of our company as a partnership built on inspiration: we provide an inspiring place to work, and we ask that employees perform their work tasks in an inspired way as well.

Building on this foundation, we've focused on the role of managers. I believe it's a privilege to manage people, and I also know that people might join an organization for its reputation or the compensation they receive, but they often leave it because of their managers. We've instituted a manager training program and delivered the curricula to all of our people managers. We've also created a new metric of manager effectiveness and begun to track managers' improvement efforts across the organization.

As I've long believed, boosting engagement and building a strong culture isn't just a matter of policies and procedures. It's about behavior. Most important, it's about how *leaders* behave, starting with me. I've always tried to take responsibility for my teams, injecting values I hold dear, such as compassion, trust, and transparency. But as I've gained more confidence and clarity in my role as CEO, and as we've focused on our culture, I now act on my values with a new awareness and sense of purpose. I try to overcommunicate, modeling transparency and trust for other managers and employees to follow. I try to take care of our people and help them feel safe. I try to engage with them in ways that will welcome them in and inspire their best work, conveying my own passion for our business and organization. I show up every day mindful of my responsibility as our culture's chief caretaker, promoter, and voice.

Our embrace of a strong people-strategy has paid off. Employee engagement has soared, with 87 percent of employees now reporting strong engagement, far above the global IT industry norm of 68 percent. The overwhelming majority of our employees feel they are given a real opportunity to improve skills (76 percent), that they are encouraged to innovate (80 percent), and that their leader—I—would keep us competing successfully (84 percent).

Our employee retention has soared, too, as has our reputation as an employer. In 2014, the *Boston Globe* named us the top large employer in the state of Massachusetts—yes, we had finally become *that* company! I'll never forget the day I found out. The organizers asked me to keep it quiet, and I just couldn't. I mean— are you kidding me, after all the work we'd put in? And best of all, since the award was based on employee opinions, we had won it because *our people* regarded us highly. I happened to be at a sales kickoff meeting that day, standing on a stage in front of 1,200-plus Kronites, and I let news of the award slip. Kronites were as excited as I was, erupting in applause.

We have since received many other honors, in some cases for multiple years running. Great Place to Work certified us as a top workplace nationally; Glassdoor honored us with its Employees' Choice award, recognizing the 100 Best Places to Work across all U.S. companies; and *Fortune* magazine named us one of its 100 Best Companies to Work For. We have also appeared on the *Forbes* list of America's Best Employers and on regional lists in Australia, Canada, China, India, and the United Kingdom.

All of this attention has sent talent surging to our doors, with applicants for open jobs rising from 32,000 in 2012 to 70,000 in 2017. As I anticipated, our talent strategy has indeed propelled our business forward. In 2014, the same year we were named best employer in our home state, we topped $1 billion in revenues, and as of 2018 we were at $1.4 billion. We have increased our revenues every year since 2009. In fact, combined with our performance before I became CEO, we've seen annual revenue growth in 19 out of the past 20 years (the exception was 2009, during the global financial crisis). And our overall value generation has been enormous, bringing exceptional investment returns for our shareholders, with the root of our value creation being our unique and engaging culture.

Beyond our top- and bottom-line growth, we have successfully completed a major, multiyear business transformation, changing from a licensed-software model to a cloud, software-as-a-service (SaaS) model—a feat that some in our industry claimed no company our size could ever pull off without seeing revenue and profit declines. As of 2018, almost all of our new customers were joining us in the Kronos Cloud. We continued to innovate at a furious pace, spending over $150 million annually on research and development, improving our industry-leading, award-winning product suites. We also introduced a pathbreaking product into the market unlike anything our industry had ever seen.

Fostering employee engagement has helped us in no small part because it has enabled us to forge stronger relationships with customers. Consider a brief example. In 2015, we suffered through one of the worst product launches in our history. A new version of our flagship product worked well for most customers, but a small number of them experienced problems. It was 100 percent our fault. In handling our customers' complaints, we applied the same practice of transparent communication that we deploy in our culture to build employee engagement. Other executives and I personally met with customers and took responsibility for the problems. "It's our fault," we told them, and we took steps to make it right. Was it easy to own up to our shortcomings? Absolutely not. But customers wrote us back after these meetings to tell us how surprising it was and what a difference it made that we were taking responsibility. As a result of our response, we strengthened relationships with many customers, turning what would normally be a highly negative situation to our benefit. Meanwhile, many of our employees felt inspired seeing us behave so honestly. "This is why I love working at Kronos," some of them told me. Even amidst the turmoil of the botched launch, their connections with our company, our leadership, and our customers deepened. Their engagement increased.

What's been most astonishing to me about our success in recent years is not so much that it happened, but *how simple* the underlying strategy has been at its core. Taking care of people first—so they can in turn delight our customers and boost our sales—isn't rocket science. *Any* company or team can do it. And yet, to my amazement, so few companies and teams actually do! Without realizing it, perhaps, leaders and managers neglect the very people who help make their businesses successful. They sometimes dismiss human resources deliverables as "soft stuff," rather than regarding the human resources department strategically. They pay lip service to culture, but don't invest time or money in cultivating it. They talk about values, but don't "walk the talk" themselves. Why is this? I just don't get it.

We need to stop taking employees for granted. Engaged employees lead to more innovative products and happier customers, which leads to stronger performance. That holds no matter your industry, and whether you're a manager overseeing a team of five or a leader running an organization of 500,000.

It isn't just customers who become happier when you prioritize employee engagement, but potentially every stakeholder with whom your company interacts. At Kronos, we apply the precepts of our culture to our business ecosystem, including customers, vendors, resellers, partners, companies we acquire, even our competitors. As we nurture strong relationships of trust and transparency with our ecosystem, we empower everyone to do their very best. That in turn allows *us* to become more successful. We now have stakeholders turning to us for advice not just on our products, but on human resources issues. Specifically, many customers have asked us to talk to their leadership teams about our culture and how to increase engagement. Remember, we're not an HR consultancy, but a software company!

I've written this book to inspire leaders and managers to build cultures of their own in which people love to work, and to provide them with some insights and tools to get started. Each chapter presents a principle that we've deployed to nurture engagement and help people "work inspired." These principles— most of which are pieces of wisdom I have discovered during my career—cover a lot of ground. They include communicating with employees so they feel safe and valued; showing respect for local cultures across geographies; fostering innovation; empowering employees to take care of their families; and helping employees behave authentically and have *fun* at work. These principles don't constitute definitive answers or formulas for engagement, but I'm confident that they will help guide as you move toward caring for your people better and motivating them more than ever.

If you don't have time for a lengthy read, no problem—I've organized the book so that you can consult each chapter independently. These chapters rely primarily on stories and examples from inside our company to illustrate my points, large and small. I also discuss an array of programs and policies we've created to build engagement and galvanize our workforce, and I focus on the leadership behaviors that inspire people to love where they work and perform at their best. I strongly believe that what we as leaders and managers do each day counts as much as policies and procedures. Each of us must take responsibility for safeguarding the culture, one personal interaction, e-mail, or public gesture at a time. If we do, we set a process in motion that, over time, instills values and practices throughout the organization.

There are no shortcuts to building a workplace environment that people love. It takes time, energy, and focus. If you're like me, you'll make mistakes along the way—plenty of them. Also, as much as you try, you'll never get it perfect. One of our employees wrote of having the "best job ever" on the website Glassdoor but also acknowledged that "every company has some warts."[1] That's very true! The important thing, though, is to commit yourself to taking this journey with your team or organization. What might *your* business look like if your employees felt proud of your company, loved what they did, and regarded the organization's mission and values as their own? What might it look like if your people trusted one another and looked out for one another, if *everyone* at all levels felt inspired to innovate every day, and if your midlevel managers empowered every employee to develop and make the most of his or her career? All this and more is possible. Do what we did: *focus on your people.* This book shows you how.

1

Become an Un-Leader

When I was a kid growing up in a small, middle-class town in New York State, our family once spotted the legendary comedian Bob Hope strolling through an airport terminal. He was a huge celebrity at the time, appearing in movies and TV comedy specials. We were thrilled to see him in real life.

As my sister remembers, our father urged her to approach Mr. Hope and say hello. "I don't want to," she told our father, "he's a celebrity."

"No," our father said, "he's just a regular person." Our father insisted that she go up to say hello, so she did. She had nothing to fear, and nothing to be embarrassed about, just because he was Bob Hope and she was a kid.

Small as it was, that episode captured so much of how my parents saw the world, and in turn, how my siblings and I were raised. To my parents, who were the children of Jewish immigrants from Eastern Europe, it didn't matter how modest a person's circumstances were. That person was just as important as the Bob Hopes of this world. And the Bob Hopes were not gods, but regular, imperfect human beings, like you and me. You don't put a person on a pedestal just because he or she has achieved great things. You admire a person's accomplishments, but you also admire *everyone* for what he or she has done in life. Each of us has achieved something important, even if it is just going to school and doing our jobs and raising our kids as best we can. That, to my parents, was worth celebrating, too.

In keeping with these beliefs, my parents expected my four siblings and me to show humility toward others. This was a non-negotiable rule. My family enjoyed a middle-class lifestyle—my father ran a small neighborhood plumbing supply store my grandfather had started. Yet during my childhood, and especially during my elementary and middle-school years, we were surrounded by people who had less than us, many of whom were immigrants. We were *never* allowed to flaunt our possessions or status. Once, a classmate came to our house, and she was surprised to learn we had a bathtub. Her family only had a shower. As my mother made clear, we weren't to mention our two bathrooms to her because that might make her feel bad. Our family was no better than hers—and we had to act that way.

As an adult, I cherish the lesson of humility my parents taught, not least because of its relevance for leading an organization or managing a team. In organizations large and small, you often see leaders exploiting their status and power to make themselves feel good. They are keenly aware of their titles, and they get an ego rush out of being in charge. Invariably, these leaders demand more respect than they give, justifying the imbalance in their minds by pointing to their lofty position.

There's nothing wrong with taking pride in your accomplishments, and there are certainly many ways to succeed as a leader.

But if you've elected, as we have, to leverage your people as a strategic business asset, then bolstering your own status and position around employees isn't your best move. Let's face it, egotistical, self-interested, or self-absorbed leaders of any stripe usually don't inspire people very much. These leaders might elicit fear, respect, or admiration, but not affection. And you need affection if you're going to spur employees to pour their hearts into their work every single day.

If there's one principle that has helped Kronos create an engaging culture in which people can feel inspired about their work, it's humility. Affording your staff the same dignity and respect as you, regardless of their status, underlies anything else you might do personally or organizationally to create an environment where people love what they do. To shift the culture of your team or organization, start here, now, with your own attitudes and behavior. Then put structures in place to help the organization as a whole make the shift.

YOU ARE NOT THE COMPANY

There's a name for the kind of humble CEO I aspire to be. I'll call him or her the "Un-Leader." If you're a CEO, please feel free to borrow it and spread it around. No matter where in an organization you reside, try regarding yourself as an "Un-Vice President," an "Un-General Manager," an "Un-Sales Supervisor," and so on.

Let's unpack the mentality that defines "Un-Leaders." First, such leaders *appreciate that their team or organization's success doesn't all owe to their personal efforts.* Some executives and managers like to think they're indispensable. But Un-Leaders harbor no illusions about the unique value of their own contributions. As CEO of Kronos, I think of myself as just another team member.

As I see it, the reason we have thousands of people in our organization is because we *need* thousands of people. It isn't all about me, nor is it about other highly visible members of our leadership team. Kronites might enjoy varying degrees of responsibility and receive different compensation, but we are all fundamentally the same in that we all bear responsibility for Kronos's success.

If you as a people manager accept that you're not above other employees, then chances are you won't take yourself as seriously as many leaders do. Some leaders form their identities around their company or their title. They are not Un-Leaders. A second feature of Un-Leaders' mentality is *an ability to put their work and their title in perspective.*

I didn't dream of becoming a CEO as a kid, nor was I groomed for the position as an adult. As I've related, my brother Mark founded Kronos, and in 1979 I came on board fresh out of college. I did everything for our start-up business, from marketing to customer service to janitorial. When a delivery arrived, I was the one who unloaded it. On weekends, I made service calls to customers.

I also spent a lot of time in sales. In the early days, I pounded the pavement, trying to convince anyone who would listen to install our product. One of our first customers was a fast-food restaurant in Chicago with 45 employees. I got to know the owner, who wanted to upgrade his Kronos system. The only time he was available was 4:30 on a Sunday morning in between pay periods. "OK," I said, "I'll do it." I remember it was a brutally cold day, 20 degrees below zero Fahrenheit. I showed up as the restaurant was opening, and the manager turned on the griddle so that I could warm my hands. Another time, I got a call from a nursing home for a meeting with its board of directors. I was 23 and didn't know what a "board of directors" was. I was nervous. It ended up being four Jewish guys in their seventies. They sat there drinking schnapps and vodka. All they wanted to do was shoot the breeze about who I was and where I was from. Finally, I said that I needed to go home, and that we'd pick another time to show them what Kronos did—I'd had too much to drink. "You seem like a nice guy," they said. "You've answered our questions—we'll buy from you!"

As the years passed, I worked my way up, but I didn't think much about becoming CEO. For decades, we at Kronos paid little attention to career development or succession planning. Early on, we were working day-to-day, month-to-month, and year-to-year to succeed. After we'd established ourselves, we continued to assume that Mark would be CEO indefinitely. And in fact, he served as CEO for almost 30 years! When he stepped down, some referred to him as the longest-running founder leading a technology company in the state of Massachusetts. It wasn't until Mark decided that he wanted to retire that we began talking seriously about succession, and that I began to think about taking over Mark's role.

I became CEO in 2005, and although I was thrilled to lead, the transition didn't come without bumps. For the first six months, my decision making wasn't crisp. I kept turning to others for advice and approval when facing tough decisions. Finally, I said to myself: "You're the CEO. You have to *act* like one by making decisions!" So I did.

Since then, I've acted decisively to implement my vision for the company, including our strategy of fully unleashing our people as a valuable asset. But I like to think that I haven't let the power of my position go to my head. In social situations, I rarely volunteer that I'm CEO of Kronos. I say that I "work in software" or that I'm "with Kronos." I might reveal my job title at some point, but people have to ask lots of questions to pull it out of me.

The truth is I don't really want to be known or remembered as a CEO. I'd much rather that people know me as a good dad, husband, or friend. That's easy to say, but I'm serious! If, for some reason, I had to step down as CEO, I'd feel sad, but life would go on. I'd have plenty to do to keep busy, and I'd feel happy and fulfilled. Being a CEO doesn't define how I think about myself. As a result, I don't spend a lot of time obsessing over my title, my authority, my power. Instead, like every other Un-Leader out there, I have more time and energy to think about what really drives the business forward: employees and customers.

HUMILITY IS POWER

A cynic might say, "Here's a guy who is just not into being CEO. He doesn't feel comfortable in the role." I understand that perception, but it's not true. I'm very comfortable being the CEO, and I'm perfectly willing to wield power when I need to, making bold decisions like taking our company private, investing in a new product initiative, going global, or transitioning our business model to the cloud. But even as I continue to steer the organization toward my vision, I remain true to my personal motivations. My goal isn't to get my way for its own sake, or to have others acknowledge my authority. Rather, it's to serve our people and promote my vision so that our culture becomes stronger and our company succeeds. That's it!

A skeptic might also object that by expressing humility, I relinquish power and risk becoming a pushover. After all, it's a dog-eat-dog world out there. Leaders who don't aggressively stake out their territory and assert their dominance will have others trample on them. If I've succeeded as CEO, these readers might speculate, it's despite my conscious efforts at humility, not because of them.

That line of thinking is likewise incorrect. As an Un-Leader, I wield *more* power than more ego-driven executives. Consider the process we deploy when acquiring other companies. In 2011, we bought Principal Decision Systems International (PDSI), a firm with about 65 employees that specialized in scheduling software for the public safety market. Since the company was performing well, we elected to let leaders there operate it largely as they had been, with our input. As CEO, I could have easily ignored PDSI and its employees, viewing my time as too important to spend on such a small part of our business. But as an Un-Leader, I didn't think that way. From the very beginning, I connected periodically with Greg, PDSI's founder and former CEO, who was continuing to run the company as a Kronos division. I also created a video to welcome employees. And several months after our acquisition, I supported Greg and former PDSI employees by appearing at their division's user group meeting, where hundreds of customers had gathered. Arriving early that day, I spoke at length with Greg, learning all kinds of details about the company and its customers. When I addressed customers and employees, I warmly welcomed them into the Kronos family, making specific references to PDSI's people and products.

As Greg remembers, PDSI employees felt skittish about becoming part of Kronos. Alongside the efforts of other Kronos executives, the attention I paid the company helped win its employees over. They came away feeling "absolutely welcome," in Greg's words. All along, I tried to make it clear how much PDSI meant to Kronos, and how important it was to us to have them on our team. That message made all the difference to them. Although many tech firms fail to keep new talent on board when they acquire other companies, the majority of PDSI employees remain Kronites today. That includes Greg, who today helps us welcome other new companies, large and small, into the Kronos family.

When we lead people, we often underestimate our emotional impact on them. Employees scrutinize us all the time—not just listening to the words we speak, but attending to all facets of our behavior, including our body language. When we are humble, and when we project that humility outwardly in our behavior, team members notice. They come to feel that their leaders respect them, are dedicated to their welfare, and are approachable. Over time, they perceive a deeper sense of kinship that they couldn't feel if their leaders existed on some elevated plane.

Led by a humble leader, employees become far more willing to open up to their boss, person to person. Do you ever sense that your people are withholding important information—that you don't know what's *really* going on? It may be that your people feel uncomfortable communicating. They don't trust you because to them, you're different. Inaccessible. Unapproachable. You're The Boss, and it feels scary to be themselves around you. So they keep silent, and you remain ignorant about important facets of the business, not knowing what you don't know. Over time, that lack of knowledge takes a significant toll.

Don't be The Boss. Be a human being. Invite your team members in by staying humble and putting them on your level.

It's ironic, isn't it? The more leaders and managers focus on their titles, the more they *limit* their influence. Feeling powerful and *being* powerful are two very different beasts. And contenting yourself with feeling powerful amounts to a wasted opportunity. Why not take advantage of the goodwill, trust, and heightened communication you engender by simply putting others on the same plane as you? It doesn't cost you anything. In fact, it's a much easier way to manage and lead. As an Un-Leader, I don't have to think about conducting myself differently depending on who I'm with. I don't worry about whether I receive all of the respect or perks or deference traditionally accorded to a CEO. I don't work as hard to make myself likeable in the eyes of employees. More power with less effort—what could be better than that?

THE UN-LEADER IN ACTION

To wield influence as an Un-Leader, you can't just think like one. You have to act like one. Many day-to-day leadership behaviors allow you to project humility and put people on your level. While some of them might feel uncomfortable or unfamiliar at first, none are complicated. You just have to decide to do them! Here are a few to focus on first:

Behavior #1: Forgo Special Perks

If you're a senior leader, do you insist on taking private planes or traveling first class on commercial airlines? Many C-level executives do. I know because I belong to various CEO groups, and when I attend meetings of these groups, I sometimes spot fellow members boarding the plane and settling into their oversized first-class seats. Before travelers in coach have made their way to their seats, these CEOs have their drink in hand and are deliberating whether to order the pasta or the chicken. Not me. I pass through first class and into coach. Could I always fly first class if I wanted to? Of course. But I'm an Un-Leader. Kronites know that I fly coach just like they do, and that parity means something. It tells them I'm no more special than they are—that I recognize everyone's worth.

I'm not saying Un-Leaders should *never* fly first class. The point is to live by the same rules as everyone else. If employees have to fly coach, then you should, too. Given how much I travel, I sometimes do get bumped up to first class. In these situations, I'll take the first-class ticket. That's fine—I'm still playing by the same rules as other Kronites. But on occasions when I'm bumped up and I happen to spot a fellow Kronite on a flight, I might trade seats with the Kronite. Can you imagine what an impression it makes on an employee to have the CEO gift you his first-class seat?

Forgoing perks and playing by the same rules as others extends beyond air travel. I don't stay in luxury hotels when I travel on business (unless that's where everyone else is staying). I don't have a window office, because no leaders in our headquarters do. And I don't get free lunch at the cafeteria in our corporate offices. I'm no better than our employees. If they pay for lunch, then so do I.

Behavior #2: Give Others the Limelight

When you're in a meeting, it's tempting to take credit, drawing attention away from your team members. Un-Leaders do the opposite. They look for opportunities to pump up others' contributions and stature. As a member of my executive team tells me, I have been known to spotlight the expertise of Kronites when introducing them to customers, prospects, vendors, and other partners. I also tend to pick junior-level Kronites in meetings I attend and tout their role, responsibility, and achievements. I solicit their opinions, too, asking questions and listening carefully. When I give formal speeches, I take the opportunity to draw attention to small teams or groups throughout the company, including new employees who recently came on board during acquisitions. These gestures take virtually no extra time and effort. You just have to get in the habit of doing them.

Behavior #3: Show Gratitude

Another way to project humility is to thank people repeatedly, even in difficult situations. Like most companies, we hold annual budgeting meetings as part of our strategic planning process. These meetings aren't always easy. Sometimes people disagree on key decisions, and tempers flare. The junior people on the finance team who run the numbers sometimes feel a bit roughed up, even though they didn't do anything wrong. Sensing this, I turn to them at the end of the meeting and publicly thank them for all their hard work. I do this no matter how rancorous the meeting gets. It's not only the executives making the final decisions who matter. The junior-level people worked hard, and they deserve to be thanked. When that gratitude comes from the mouth of the CEO, or from that of a midlevel manager leading a team, it sends a clear signal not just about the value that every Kronite brings but also about the importance of humility in our culture.

Behavior #4: Remember Basic Respect

We're all busy, deluged by e-mails and meetings. It's easy to forget basic courtesies, especially when it comes to frontline employees. Take some deep breaths and make it a priority to show respect for everyone. Hold the door. If you're in a meeting and getting coffee for yourself, ask others if they want some, including the 22-year-old intern. If you're walking with junior employees down the hallway, don't walk ahead of them, but side by side. If you're holding a meeting with your team, don't sit at the head of the conference table every time. If you're in an elevator with a group of people, look up from your phone and say hello. If you're in a cab or a restaurant, talk to the people serving you. Ask them about their lives and thank them for their efforts. Practiced daily, little gestures like these make a big difference. And again, they send a message.

Behavior #5: Get—and Stay—in the Weeds

Some leaders believe they should focus on the high-level strategy, leaving it to others lower in the organization to perform more mundane tasks like interacting with customers and handling their complaints. That thinking is ridiculous. We have teams of sales and service people who care for our customers day-to-day, and as CEO I don't micromanage. But I do frequently step in and interact personally with customers to address problems and gauge their satisfaction. In 2015, when customers complained about glitches in our flagship product, I worked with many members of our customer service team to resolve the problem, even though other executives in our organization were already involved. Over a period of months, I followed up with these employees, making sure that they and other teams in our organization were fixing the problems. Because I involved myself directly, frontline Kronites felt empowered. They knew that senior leadership understood their concerns and was taking action. They also got the underlying message: as CEO, I'm not too high up or important to concern myself with their work. Managers at any level can send a similar message. Spend as much time as possible in the trenches and get your hands dirty. Employees will notice.

Behavior #6: Admit When You Don't Know

As an Un-Leader, I strive to remain keenly aware of the limits of my own knowledge. This opens up a space for fellow Kronites to come forth with their own solutions. Our culture becomes more innovative—a theme I'll develop in Chapter 13.

As an organization, we've also become adept at recognizing our own limitations, and that has helped us immensely. In 2015, when we were developing an innovative new product, we didn't assume that we knew everything. We assumed the opposite and brought in a series of outside consultants—customer advisors who met with us every few months during the design phase—to critique our new product and suggest improvements. Most people want to believe that their baby is beautiful, and it's hard to stomach criticism or acknowledge imperfections. But in this case, the feedback—which included the need to improve the product's appearance, functionality, responsiveness, and overall design—allowed us to launch a superior product. In one instance, customers told us that it was too difficult to add or schedule an employee and to edit an employee record. It took us a few months to handle feedback like this, but we adjusted the product accordingly, and the end result was much better.

Behavior #7: Solicit Feedback

Most leaders and managers know they're supposed to give feedback, critiquing employees on their performance. But think about what it means when you turn the tables and ask others for feedback on your performance. Did *they* get out of a meeting with you what they had hoped? Did you deliver the guidance *they* needed? Did your reasoning make sense to *them*? By posing these questions, you're again putting yourself on the same plane as everyone else. And you're getting valuable feedback that can help you improve.

When I run meetings, I typically go around the room, asking people for their views before taking action. You might wonder whether people will readily communicate unpleasant truths I need to hear. I admit, there's no guarantee that they will. But in keeping with our culture's emphasis on trust (Chapter 3), I choose to take for granted that my people will be open and honest with me. And in fact, I do receive critical feedback all the time from others around me. Every week, executives or managers will make comments like: "You need to speak differently in front of this group," or "I don't think the meeting you led was all that successful." Such feedback has led me to change my position on how I lead meetings, how I treat customers, or whom I hire for critical positions.

Ultimately, much of what our senior leadership team decides at Kronos doesn't just reflect my ideas but is rather a direct result of employee feedback. That extends to all sorts of decisions big and small. For example, the appearance of our workstations, common spaces, and furniture in our headquarters reflects employee feedback. We had three or four manufacturers of workspaces set up their products. We didn't tell employees who the vendors were, but we asked them to sit in the spaces and vote on them. About 800 Kronites cast their votes. We made our selection based on what people said they liked best.

THREE STEPS TO A HUMBLER ORGANIZATION

Modeling humility can go a long way toward shifting the culture of your team or organization and building engagement. To take it further, the organization can codify humble behavior, integrating it formally into its culture. Several years ago, when we were transforming ourselves into a company with cloud offerings, we set forth key desired behaviors for Kronites everywhere to focus on and embrace. One of these was humility. As we defined it, humility meant assuming "positive intent" and competence on the part of others, engaging others by asking questions and listening, and putting your own "agenda aside to operate in the best interests of the customer and company." We also clarified that humility and "bold" leadership were not opposites, but rather went hand in hand.

Precisely how you define humility for your people is up to you. What's important is to:

1. Set a baseline standard with your own behavior
2. Lay out clear, formal expectations about how people throughout the organization are to behave
3. Infuse policies and processes with an ethic of humility

Our human resources department provides incentives to Kronites who refer new hires. We used to offer greater incentives for executive-level hires than for lower-level hires. Now we pay the same incentives for every hire. Why should we send the message that executives count more than other employees? Likewise, under our open time off policy (Chapter 9), Kronites, irrespective of their title or seniority, receive the same treatment when it comes to time off. We trust each of them to put in the time required to do their jobs well, and also take the time off they need to stay happy and healthy.

Imagine what you could accomplish if you removed the psychological distance separating you and other leaders from your employees. Imagine if other managers and executives in your organization followed your example so that humility became an entrenched part of the culture. That's happened over the past decade at Kronos, and it has made it far easier for us to take other steps to change our culture, boost engagement, and become a billion-dollar company.

My parents had it right all those years ago: every human being counts equally. So the next time you meet someone in a social situation, try something different. Don't blurt out your title. Tell them you work "in software," "in retail," "in manufacturing," or whatever business you may be in. Small actions really do mean a lot.

2

Overcommunicate

One morning, I was strolling through our lobby when I spotted a woman in her thirties. She was sitting in a chair, checking her phone. From her badge, I could tell that she was a Kronite, but I hadn't met her before. Since I was passing right by her, I stopped and started a conversation. "Having a good morning?" I asked. "What do you think of our new offices? What's your favorite part?" I lobbed more friendly questions at her, and we chatted for a few minutes before I said goodbye and headed toward the elevators. I never identified myself as the CEO, and I don't think she knew. My goal was simply to learn a little bit from her, find out what was on her mind, what she wanted out of her job, and how she saw the company.

I have encounters like this all the time—while I'm riding the elevator, while I'm standing in line at the cafeteria, as I'm walking to my car. I chat with everyone: employees, customers, prospective employees, vendors who happen to be visiting our offices. There's a Yiddish word for this behavior: *kibitzing*. During my childhood, my mother joked that my father's plumbing business was really a community center, all these customers coming in and hanging around. She used to chide my father, saying, "I don't know how you make a living, because all you do is *kibitz*." She was right. My father sold his share of PVC pipe, but he was also constantly bantering with his customers, learning about their struggles and concerns, helping if he could.

> **Kibitz** (def): To chat, converse

Source: American Heritage Dictionary[1]

At Kronos, I think of myself as the *kibitzer*-in-chief, and I recommend kibitzing to you as a powerful means of building a more engaged and inspired team or workforce. Like expressions of humility on the part of leaders and managers, short, personal conversations with employees are seemingly inconsequential acts that over time pay huge dividends. CEOs of billion-dollar companies tend to converse primarily with their carefully chosen leadership team, and nobody else. They satisfy themselves with getting up on a stage and lecturing employees about the company, its strategies, its values, delegating most other communications with employees to the public relations or human resources departments. To inspire people and create a workplace they cherish, I believe you must build personal relationships with them and establish a culture throughout the company of open and honest communication. Communicating frequently with employees and other stakeholders, preferably face-to-face, can help you accomplish both objectives. In fact, don't just communicate—*over*communicate. You really can't do it enough!

THE FINE ART OF KIBITZING

Kibitzing might sound funny to your ear, but it has long had its place in organizations, encapsulated in the well-known practice of "management by walking around." Yet not everybody does such informal chatting correctly. As a leader or manager, you can't just spend time mingling with frontline employees and talking with them about their work. For the best results, you have to *ask plenty of questions, and really listen to employees' responses.*

As I go about my day, I ask employees a variety of open-ended questions about their work and personal lives, simple queries like, "What are you working on?" "How was your weekend?" "How is your family?" I pose these questions to most Kronites I meet, whether at our headquarters or when traveling to other locations because I truly care about them and what they're doing. These employees in turn are sometimes shocked that their CEO would take a minute or two to acknowledge them as human beings because relatively few leaders or managers do. Likewise, when I attend industry or customer events, I seek out people at all levels with whom to chat, not identifying my title and asking them about their families, hobbies, and so on. When they later discover that they were speaking to the CEO of Kronos, they gain a new appreciation for our company as a friendly, engaging, and humble partner with whom to do business.

The practices I've described so far are entry-level *kibitzing*. Let's take it to the next level. I'm not perfect, but I try very hard to remember details. After meeting someone for the first time and then seeing them again months or years later, I try to recall something about them, perhaps asking a question such as, "Is your father feeling better?" or "How did your son's twelfth birthday party go?" or "How is your daughter enjoying college?" I've realized that these follow-up queries mean a lot to people. It helps that I happen to have a good memory for names and details, in part because as an extrovert I enjoy these encounters so much. If you're more introverted, or if you have a bad memory, no worries. Try jotting down quick notes to keep track of the employees you meet. It might take a bit more effort, but it's worth it.

Speaking of "worth it," the benefits of frequent, casual conversation go well beyond creating a culture of engagement or helping to build our brand as a people-friendly company. When chatting with employees, I gain new insights into our business that I never would have learned otherwise—details about struggles teams are having, new opportunities that are cropping up in various corners of our company, big victories that teams have notched, and so on. Just as valuable, I gain an intuitive sense for the personalities, needs, and desires of our employees. Over time, I forge personal relationships, creating a general atmosphere of free-flowing communication. Employees feel more comfortable coming to me with their problems or concerns, which affords me new opportunities to help drive our business forward. I can't tell you how often employees consult me for help with a customer or for a quick e-mail introduction to a member of my personal network and so on. I respond to all of these requests and help whenever I can.

Some might view these requests as distractions that prevent me from doing other work. I agree, they absolutely are—but they're *good* distractions. Why should everyone else but me take responsibility for driving our business forward day-to-day? If I can help smooth the path to a new business deal by sending an e-mail, or if I can inspire a team by recording a five-minute video, I'm happy to do that. In general, casual conversation doesn't add much time to your daily routine. *Right now, all those moments when you're walking to your car or riding the elevator are wasted, from a business standpoint.* They're not producing anything. If you use those moments to help engage employees, then you're helping to build, sustain, and mobilize your business's greatest asset: your people.

As managers of people, we can derive even more value from casual conversations, using them proactively to overcome issues as they arise. When I'm mulling over a business problem, I often stroll the hallways, asking the opinion of several employees whom I happen to encounter. These impromptu "focus groups" give me valuable insight into what our workforce is thinking and real-time access to our employees' creative talents. I also perform what I call "micro-communication" throughout the day, popping in on employees for brief, two- or three-minute conversations. I might ask their input on an issue I'm working on or bounce new ideas off of them. At the end of the day, I'll mentally review multiple conversations, noticing patterns in what I've heard and using that information to help make decisions. This process has become a regular and indispensable part of my daily work routine.

You might wonder: can the tactic of casual conversations work in a global culture? Absolutely. When I visit our facilities in locations around the world, I always tour the space and shake hands with employees, sometimes spending several hours with them. During my visits, I'll go with our local leadership to visit customers, prospects, and partners, seeing what our employees are seeing. I might not speak the language of the people I meet, but by asking open-ended questions, I usually manage to forge a personal connection. At the end of each day, I'll write short notes to customers or prospects whom I met. These notes incorporate details I learned during my meetings or refer to topics we discussed. When I'm in China, I'll send notes I write in English to a member of our team there, who translates them into Mandarin and sends them back to me to send from my own e-mail account.

Customers and prospects really appreciate the personal touch, all the more so because they're reading it in their own language.

Casual conversations need not include actual personal interactions to feel meaningful to people. You can conduct these conversations virtually, using tools such as e-mail and social media. The head of one of our international offices recently sent a picture with a caption reading, "Cheers from London." He noted that the Kronite in the photo was about to be recognized for the fifteenth time at our annual "Legend Makers" sales recognition getaway. In the 30 seconds it took me to respond, I cemented in a small way my relationship with this leader. By reading this message, I also learned a bit about what these leaders were up to, and I learned some information about our longtime salesperson. The next time I encountered this salesperson, I could surprise him by congratulating him on his Legend Makers achievement. *Holy cow,* he might think, *how did Aron know that?* Thanks to this 30-second interaction, I could touch two people, one of whom—the salesperson—might well mention our encounter to other employees, magnifying the impact. Forget that "forward" button—let's click "reply" instead! It may not work for every people manager, but I've found it helpful to show my appreciation, one "trivial" interaction at a time.

TAKING CONVERSATION TO THE MASSES

No matter how communicative you might be one-on-one, you can't forge a personal connection with everyone if you run a large team or organization. What do you do, especially if you lead a global organization? One solution is to *lean on other leaders and managers to help you make connections with employees.* Members of our leadership team have become more proactive about getting out there and talking to people in their own organizations. A number of midlevel Kronite managers have told me that they've begun to spend more time conversing casually with their team members because they've seen me do it. Hold casual conversations with employees often enough, and it becomes embedded in the culture, with masses of frontline employees touched by it.

You can move along this process of culture building, and also build surprisingly personal connections with masses of employees all at once, by *turning to mass communications*. I strive to overcommunicate using every digital medium at my disposal. Frequently during the year, I send out companywide e-mails with personal messages from me. I also create "aron@ work" videos, short, low-budget blogs that capture me speaking impromptu about company performance, year-end objectives, product launches—whatever is on my mind. When I say low budget, I mean I use an iPad, recording the blogs in one take. If I stumble on my words, that's OK. The lack of polish doesn't hurt. On the contrary, it gives employees the sense of an authentic, rough-cut message from me. The point of these videos is to help Kronites feel engaged and give them a window into my thinking. Our employees in locales around the world tell me how much they appreciate these messages as a way to feel part of the Kronos family.

Social media is another important tool in the overcommunicator's toolbox. So many CEOs I meet grimace when I ask them about their social media activity. "Ugh, no," they say. "Why would I do *that?*" I think, and sometimes respond, "Social media is such a useful way to project a personal presence across distances." In addition to well-known external social media platforms, we use an internal collaboration platform that enables Kronites to share information, ask and answer questions, congratulate one another on personal milestones, and work together to solve customer challenges. I frequently hop on threads of conversation. In 2018, one of our leaders was named to a prestigious "Forty Under 40" list in a regional publication. Our public relations team posted a message about it, congratulating him. The following day, I posted a comment, tagging the Kronite who won that distinction. "Holy Macaroni!" I said. "Congratulations. So proud of you . . . big hug." I wanted to recognize this stellar Kronite and show other Kronites that we're engaged with their work, and that we're listening and responding in a direct and authentic way.

We deploy a range of other tactics to help managers throughout our organization listen to employees. We closely monitor comments on social media channels, looking at how people rate us and the comments they leave. Watching and listening to what is posted on social media helps us understand better what people want out of the companies they work for, and how our employees perceive Kronos.

We also rely on our employee engagement surveys to gauge employees' perspectives on how our organization is run. We conduct a full employee engagement survey once each year, following that up six months later with a "pulse" survey (a shorter version of the engagement survey). Many companies field these surveys, but not all of them take them as seriously as we do. Our survey, which over 90 percent of Kronites globally fill out, yields tremendous insights into our organization's strengths and weaknesses. In addition to their responses to quantitative questions, employees can also leave qualitative comments about their team and departments, including changes they'd like to see. Leaders and managers throughout the organization process the feedback, implementing meaningful improvements, including enhancements to our products, ideas for strengthening our employee experience, and much more.

In 2016, for instance, the head of our finance department addressed a few "problem" areas identified by survey participants, including IT tools that some felt were difficult to use, inadequate recognition of employees, and the need for more information about career advancement in the department. For each area, this leader assigned someone to champion the initiative and required managers to submit action plans and quarterly progress updates. Within 12 months, there was "notable progress" in the department's recognition of employees, and the programs implemented to address these issues were well received and highly utilized. We have found that when employees see their leaders taking action, and when they spot evidence of real change, they feel valued and listened to. The sense of a meaningful and ongoing organizational conversation deepens.

To help foster two-way conversations and listening throughout the organization, we offer employees optional training on an array of communication skills. One course we offer, "Courageous Conversations," shows Kronites how to stay calm and communicate effectively when broaching difficult issues, even when they're anxious or upset. Other courses train Kronites in how to deliver feedback in helpful ways, how to persuade others to take action even when you don't wield formal authority over them, and how to get results in high-stakes situations through communication.

In addition to training, we mobilize an array of formal venues at the team and department levels to encourage active communication, including all-employee meetings, internal blogs, roundtables, question-and-answer sessions, and the like. These venues aren't meaningless schedule-cloggers—they make a real difference. In 2012, one of our sales leaders created a Sales Management Council (SMC), composed of 12 of our top sales managers, which would allow them to offer members of our executive committee direct feedback on what was and wasn't working in the field. With confidentiality assured, members could speak openly without fear of retribution. In 2016, the SMC spent two days outlining how leadership could better support sales reps in the field and empower them to impact deals and exceed customer demands. For instance, our cloud customers had been asking for exceptions to the usual terms and conditions in our contracts, and members of our leadership team were routinely making the same changes. Our sales reps wanted the latitude to make these common contract adjustments on their own, without having to undergo the cumbersome process of obtaining approval.

During the two-day session, SMC members challenged and debated with leaders, distinguishing between customer requests that were very common and shouldn't require leadership approval and those that weren't so common and did. The SMC described the kinds of customer negotiations in which having the ability to make a quick decision without approval would not only facilitate a deal but enhance customers' impressions of us as a company. Our leaders spent time helping the SMC understand the reasons why a requested change might require special approval, and what might happen if a sales rep made the wrong decision with a customer. After this session, our SMC presented the resulting recommendations to our chief revenue officer. He in turn presented them to our executive team, which wound up approving every recommendation. The field sales team gained the authority to offer more options to customers than they previously had, as well as the ability to make quick decisions during the sales process as they saw fit. These changes signaled to the field that our leadership was behind them, listening to their feedback and looking for opportunities to support them.

You might think that all of this communication is excessive. Don't I have more important things to do? I really don't. Our people matter most, and they *want* us to communicate, more than they want just about anything else. I'll never forget a study I encountered decades ago. Researchers surveyed a large group of managers, asking them to list the topics that they believed employees regarded as most important. Most managers cited factors like compensation or job security. When researchers queried employees, pay was pretty far down their list. The most important factor for them was, you guessed it, good communication. That stuck with me, and I believe it holds true today. In the 2017 Great Places to Work Trust Index survey, 96 percent of Kronites surveyed found that we "often" or "almost always" delivered "great communication."[2] That's a big deal. Employees value when you share information with them, especially information that they're surprised to receive. I don't recall if employees in that older study indicated how they felt about managers who listened, but I'd be shocked if they didn't heartily approve of that, too. Don't underestimate the value of communication. Chances are, you don't do it nearly enough.

THEY CAN HANDLE THE TRUTH

Several years ago, I hired a new leader to run one of our company's largest departments staffed by hundreds of Kronites. We had performed our usual screening process, including seven months of interviews, "backdoor" reference checks, and other strict vetting. I oversaw the process, and most leaders on our executive committee had interviewed the hire. Yet after only six weeks on the job, it was clear—our new hire was not working out. I had to let him go, so I did. Afterward, I swallowed my pride and called our board members individually to deliver the news and take responsibility. Many of them were surprised, yet strangely, quite complimentary. "You rock," they told me.

I couldn't believe my ears. "Really," I said, "I rock?"

They told me they had never seen a CEO fess up so readily upon making a significant hiring mistake, and they commended me for the swiftness of my decision. When I told Kronites in this department that we had made a hiring error, they, too, expressed gratitude that we moved swiftly to make things right. I didn't understand this reaction. Why was I getting so much credit here? How could I *not* have openly admitted my mistake and taken steps to remedy it?

There's little point in overcommunicating with employees and other stakeholders if you aren't prepared to communicate truthfully and transparently. I don't know what life is like at other companies—I've spent my whole career at Kronos—but I hear that leaders sometimes aren't so truthful or transparent. Really? Are you *kidding me*? That's incredible. How can leaders hope to build personal relationships with employees and inspire them if they're constantly evading, downplaying, hiding, manipulating, or distorting the truth?

It's easy to communicate honestly when business is going well, much harder when it's not. But leaders and organizations must strive for transparency at all times. Perhaps the greatest test of my commitment to open communication came in 2009, when we had to let go more than 250 Kronites. We had just experienced our first year-on-year decline in quarterly revenues, and in a weak and highly uncertain economy, we anticipated further tightening in demand for our products. To weather these tough times, we had to realign our expenses with our revenues. We considered options such as furloughs, pay cuts, or benefit adjustments, but concluded that none of these would solve our financial problems without also causing our business significant long-term harm.

Although layoffs would hurt in the short term, we would try to do them in as humane a way as possible, giving affected Kronites generous severance and assistance finding new jobs.

Once we decided upon this course of action, I knew what I needed to do: go before our remaining Kronites in person and take them blow-by-blow through our decision-making process. January 7, 2009, the day after our layoffs took place, was the hardest day so far in my career as a leader. I stood before hundreds of our employees at a time and offered them my unscripted thoughts. "It's nobody's fault we're in the position we're in," I told them. "To lead the company responsibly and to protect the jobs of the vast majority of Kronites, we simply have to resize our workforce to our business." As I spoke, and later as I responded to numerous questions from Kronites, I watched people crying, and I myself became teary-eyed. It was excruciating to face these people who had given so much to our company, who had seen their colleagues laid off, and who worried that they might be next. But I pulled myself together and did it. I'm glad I did. Kronites seemed to appreciate my honesty with them. It didn't erase their suffering, but it at least inspired them to see that their leadership respected them enough to tell them the truth. The bonds of affection between Kronites and the company didn't break. On the contrary, they became stronger, powering us ahead as the economic crisis passed and our growth resumed.

As vital as it is at peak emotional moments, open and honest communication is just as important day in and day out—and with customers as well as employees. In 2017, I attended a summit held by one of our large global customers. Addressing the group, I acknowledged problems that had cropped up in our handling of the account. I didn't make a big deal about it, but I allowed that yes, there had been some slipups, we were taking full responsibility, and we were addressing it. Wow, did that have an impact. The next day, a Kronite thanked me for that gesture and told me what a difference it had made. She said that she loved watching the expressions on customers' faces when they heard the CEO admit that the company wasn't perfect and that it had made mistakes. "It's so unusual," she said. Really? It shouldn't be! If you're used to putting up a veneer of perfection, try owning up to your shortfalls. Your ego might take a hit at first, but it won't crumble. And customers will respect you more.

It's equally important as leaders and managers to own our failings in front of employees. During the software glitch debacle I mentioned earlier, senior leaders stood before groups of our employees and took personal responsibility for the problems we were having, apologizing to Kronites for what we had put them through and affirming that it wouldn't happen again. I personally got on the phone with our sales support team and apologized for how much work they had to do to keep our customers happy. I held multiple conference calls to make sure that everyone on the team had a chance to hear the words straight from my mouth. And I repeated the message at our annual sales kickoff, with over 1,200 Kronites in attendance. As one of our executives told me, these gestures were huge because it wasn't an outside consultant standing up and speaking honestly about a tough subject. It was the CEO.

Our leadership team takes honesty and transparency so seriously that we go to great lengths to embed it throughout the organization. Although we're a privately held company, we share our financial performance on a quarterly basis, distributing our press releases to all employees and including detailed information about revenue, earnings, and other critical measures, as well as key business developments. As I'll describe later, all Kronites receive a clear overview of the company's business strategy. We also train our managers to be honest and transparent, explicitly identifying "honest dialogue" and "sharing information openly and consistently" as core elements of our corporate leadership model. We want honest, transparent, and frequent communications to be the rule at Kronos, and that means making it a clear responsibility of middle managers, not just leaders.

CREATE A MORE WELCOMING WORKPLACE

Early in the writing of this book, our head of corporate communications proposed doing some interviews with others in the company. She thought it would help jog my memory of events, and that it might allow us to uncover inspiring stories within the company. At the very least, it would allow us to inject a variety of Kronite perspectives into the book. Why should it all be about me? And wouldn't it be cool if we could use this project as yet another opportunity to foster dialogue and build relationships? Our communications department wound up holding many interviews and focus groups, and although I did not participate directly, I did receive regular updates about what transpired.

At one of the focus groups, a young Kronite whom I'll call Charlotte participated. She had started at Kronos two years earlier as an intern, and we'd hired her on a permanent basis during her senior year of college. At the time of the focus group, she worked as a member of our industry marketing team. During the session, she recalled standing outside the elevator a few months earlier, waiting for the doors to open. I walked by, accompanied, in her words, by "a bunch of people in suits." Apparently, when I saw her, I paused, said a friendly hello, and chatted with her for a minute or two. That surprised her. As she related, "I remember thinking, OK, I'm 22 and I'm pretty sure most 22-year-olds won't meet the CEO of their company, let alone have them walk out of a group to just say, 'Hi, how are you doing? Is everything OK?'"

Think about this for a moment. Months later, a simple, friendly gesture on my part stood out in this young employee's mind. And it made a difference to her. Moreover, as she revealed later in the session, she perceived the entire company and its culture to be equally friendly, open, and welcoming. "It's a big company," she said, "and from the outside, it might seem scary, but within a day I thought, 'OK, I want to be here for a long time' . . . it's a very calm and welcoming environment . . . consistently a very positive experience all the time."

Here's a talented millennial, the kind of employee that many companies have difficulty attracting and keeping. Two years into her job, she probably couldn't be more engaged. Not because she earns a competitive salary, which she does, but because people treat her like a human being, up to and including her CEO. They communicate with her person to person, welcoming her in. They take the time to build a relationship with her.

No matter what size company or team you lead or manage, making personal connections with your employees is vital. *Really talk to people*, and enable them to have a voice as well. Walk around and chat with employees informally. Use mass communications to ensure that you connect in some way with every employee at all of your locations. Make frequent, two-way communications an organizational imperative. See to the quality of communications throughout the company, setting norms of honesty and transparency. Don't just act like you or the organization cares what employees or prospects are saying. Ask deeper, more meaningful questions about their work, family, and outside interests, and really listen, taking action when appropriate. An engaged workforce is one that communicates, in the richest, most fulfilling sense of the word. And hey, it's fun! So, before you read any further, put down this book and start kibitzing.

3

Trust Them
(Again and Again)

Early one morning in 2015, Chris, a high-performing member of my leadership team, knocked on my door. "Have a minute?"

As you know by now, I always have a minute to speak with Kronites. I invited Chris to come in and sit down.

"You'll never guess who called me," he said, cracking a smile.

"Who?" I asked.

"A recruiter. I've got to say, it's a great opportunity."

I leaned back in my chair. "Tell me about it."

A large technology company wanted Chris to consider a high-profile job opening. Chris would have to move his family to a different city, but his status and compensation would increase considerably. Chris asked me whether I thought the opportunity sounded promising enough to pursue. Would I pursue it if I were him? I told him I probably would, and suggested he agree to an interview.

Now, as a manager or leader, you might be shaking your head. Why in the world would I possibly advise one of my high performers to investigate an opportunity at another organization? Am I crazy?

No, I'm not, and I'll explain why in Chapter 11, when I describe the unusual approach to retention and career development we embrace at Kronos. (Oh, what the heck, here's a quick preview: we believe that we don't own people's careers, even if it means leaving them free to leave Kronos and pursue opportunities elsewhere.)

For now, let's address a different question. If Chris had such an attractive job opportunity, why would he have come to me, his boss, for advice? Wouldn't it have been smarter for him to keep it to himself until he was ready to make his move? For all he knew, I might have felt betrayed or fearful and moved to retaliate.

Chris came to me because he *trusted* me, and he trusted our relationship. Yes, he knew my general philosophy about retention, my belief that as employers we don't "own" people and their careers. But leaders can espouse idealistic philosophies and still act differently when confronted with a real-life choice. Chris knew from past experience that I would treat him as a friend. I wouldn't freak out upon hearing that he was interviewing somewhere else, and I would give him advice that was in *his* best interest, not the company's. Only if he actually received an offer would I put on my "Kronos" hat and do my damnedest to convince him to stay.

Deep, abiding trust among team members is vital to building an engaged workforce. It was important to Chris that we could talk honestly, and that he could trust me to take his interests to heart. He didn't feel trapped in his job, as so many people do, nor did he feel like he had to live some "secret life" at work while exploring an opportunity elsewhere. He could relax and be himself, tapping into my perspective and insight. This in turn made him more loyal and more committed to the company. Not surprisingly, he hasn't left Kronos, even though recruiters inundate his inbox with job offers. To date, he has declined two attractive offers to become CEO at other companies. Other aggressively recruited Kronites have chosen to stay, too. Across our workforce, we sustain sky-high retention levels, even in an industry as talent-hungry as ours. While all the principles discussed in this book contribute to that, trust ranks highly.

We've worked incredibly hard to instill trust throughout the organization, one manager at a time, starting with me. First, we give employees atypical degrees of latitude and freedom. Until proven otherwise, we assume their competence, judgment, and good intentions. Because we place so much faith in employees, they return the favor, placing a remarkable degree of trust in us. Their trust in turn leads to far better performance—more innovation, quicker recovery from mistakes, more energy and enthusiasm at work.

Think of how much more inspired your team members would become if you put your faith in them, if you didn't constantly look over their shoulders, if you *assumed* they were competent and would do the right thing. Think of how much better your team and organization would function if trust prevailed, with more fluid communication and quicker identification of problems as they arise. In my case, Chris's willingness to openly discuss his career possibilities allowed me to plan staffing on my team better, and it allowed me to manage him better. Because I understood his goals and challenges, I could find the right opportunities and experiences for him so that he could grow his career within Kronos—yet another way that trust supports engagement and retention.

Trusting others isn't easy, especially if your workplace has a history of strained relationships. Also, although the vast majority of employees prove worthy of your trust, a few don't, and on occasion you might have to deal with the consequences. That's OK—life isn't perfect. On the whole, the benefits of infusing trust into the culture far exceed the costs accrued when individual employees disappoint you. Bottom line: For a more engaged, higher-performing workforce, start by assuming competence, and then demonstrate to people over and over again that you trust them. Toss micromanagement out the window!

CULTIVATING TRUST AS A LEADER

As beneficial as the idea of trust might appear, it's still a pretty "soft" concept to many leaders and managers. Can individuals and organizations really nurture something as abstract as trust throughout an entire workforce? And if they can, does cultivating a culture of trust really help foster engagement and propel a team or organization forward?

Let's take these questions one at a time. Individuals and organizations most certainly can take steps to increase trust among employees. I know because I've done it as a manager, and Kronos as a whole has, too. In many cases, executives and team managers who have entered Kronos mistrusting others have become noticeably more trusting in just a few short months or years. One of our high-performing leaders didn't seem especially trusting when he first came to Kronos. That wasn't entirely a surprise. In his field, sniffing out unfavorable terms in contracts is a big part of the job. Still, over the course of a few years, I saw a clear shift in this leader's behavior—he became incredibly trusting both of me and of his own team members. He no longer assumed that only he had the best ideas. Instead, he reached out to others for input and participation. As a result, he became one of the most valuable and respected members of our leadership team.

Trust isn't something you can expect or claim for yourself. Rather, employees must choose to bestow it on you—or not. It's *theirs to give.* Leaders and managers can earn employees' trust by behaving respectfully and communicating honestly. And just as important, leaders and managers can take the first step and bestow their trust on employees. The best way to persuade people to trust you is not to lecture them about trust, but simply to trust them. That way, you establish an underlying expectation of trusting behavior, modeling what you wish to cultivate in your team, department, or entire organization.

In managing my own team, I don't just refrain from micromanaging—I trust enough to *require* independence. During the 1980s, when I oversaw our direct sales force, team members would ask to talk through a difficult decision. "Sure," I'd say. They'd describe the situation, which might have involved how to negotiate part of a contract, and they'd ask me what I thought they should do. "I don't know," I'd say.

"What do you mean you don't know?"

"Well, I haven't met the customer. You have. What do *you* think we should do?"

"Well," team members would say, "I think we should price it this way"—and then they'd describe their plans.

I'd shrug my shoulders. "Fine. Price it that way. It sounds great!"

The team members would stare at me. "So, I have your approval?"

I would smile. "Of course you have my approval. You're the expert on the ground. You're the one who knows the situation better than anyone else. I trust your decision making. Let's go for it!"

Make no mistake, I haven't devolved *all* authority to my team members. I reserve the right to overrule people when they veer off-track or to supervise work more closely. I've also held my team members accountable for their mistakes. But my default move has been to solicit employees' perspectives and let them decide. I haven't wasted a lot of time second-guessing people or assigning blame when business developments didn't work out as planned. Have I personally been burned when trusting people? Have I had to crack down on people who didn't learn from their mistakes? Absolutely! But almost always, my trust in team members has proven well founded.

As CEO, I've continued to take a largely hands-off approach to my senior team, in some cases asking them to shoulder large amounts of responsibility. When we decided to invest $150 million in Workforce Dimensions®, a new product line that we hoped would one day "put Kronos out of business" (Chapter 13), I put a small group of our senior executives in charge, giving them clear direction up front, but otherwise letting them run the project as they saw fit. I checked in every several weeks, giving feedback on the general direction and offering encouragement. Likewise, when we decided to relocate our headquarters, I charged key executives with selecting and designing the new offices, giving them some initial guidance, checking in periodically, and only making decisions on matters that I especially cared about, such as doing away with window offices for executives.

In retrospect, I've relied on my colleagues to execute just about every major strategic initiative we've attempted during my tenure as CEO. In 2009, we decided to adopt a vertical approach to selling our software. Instead of our salespeople covering geographic territories, they would sell into specific industries, like healthcare or manufacturing. We made this change because we felt our salespeople would operate more effectively if they could master the intricacies of a specific industry. Going vertical was risky. Our salespeople would have to serve new sets of customers, and we would have to structure their compensation differently. If we executed the shift poorly, morale might have suffered, impact-ing our sales. Many salespeople expressed concern when we first broached the prospect of verticalization. Would they receive the bonuses they were counting on? Could they really excel serving just one industry?

I put one of our executives, John, in charge of verticalization. He oversaw the plan's execution with little involvement from me. After analyzing the customer base for every one of our salespeople, John discovered that a single industry already accounted for 80 per-cent of a typical Kronite's sales portfolio. Armed with this data, he sat down with salespeople and showed them that for the most part, verticalization actually represented business as usual. Instead of regarding the new strategy as a threat, they started to see it as an opportunity to enhance their own effectiveness and increase their bonuses. To date, verticalization remains one of our most success-ful strategic moves, one steeped in and enabled by trust.

As CEO, I have similarly extended trust to other stakeholders, most notably our customers. I tend to be very open with custom-ers, liberally sharing information and personal anecdotes. I also have a habit of taking the customers' side during a negotiation, trusting that they won't try to take advantage of us. "You're abso-lutely right," I'll say to them, "Kronos shouldn't be requiring that of you." I'll also frequently take the customers' side during inter-nal conversations with members of our team. In one instance, a customer, a small golf course, was struggling to implement our software. After reviewing our contract, our service team concluded that we had performed as we'd promised and owed the customer nothing more in the way of free customer service. When the customer continued to complain, our service team came to me and told me of their intention to cut off the customer. I insisted that we continue to work with the customer to help the business succeed, regardless of whether our contract required it.

As I told them, our brand is all about customer success, and I'm prepared to trust that customers aren't trying to take advantage of us. This conversation made a big impression on the leader of our service team. Years later, she still talks about it. In general, when I have conversations like this in the presence of Kronos salespeople, they not only perceive a display of trust, but validation of our commitment to always do right by customers, even when it puts us in an uncomfortable or financially disadvantageous position.

Perceiving that I trust others, my team members feel more inclined to communicate freely about their own projects, initiatives, and new ideas. They also bestow trust upon their own teammates more often. That's how it works at Kronos: trust displayed at various levels of management filters through the organization, creating a general climate of mutual faith and respect.

If you manage others, start infusing trust into your culture right now. Provoke your people to come up with answers to pressing business questions rather than dictating them yourself. When you can, drop others into roles that will challenge them and build their confidence. Don't check in on your reports every two minutes. When mistakes occur, don't go ballistic. Hold people accountable, but then frame mistakes as "growth opportunities," giving people the opportunity to mature and achieve stronger results in the future.

INSTITUTIONALIZING TRUST

If you run an organization or team, you have the power to create broader, more formal mechanisms to instill trust. Here are several important techniques we use at Kronos:

Set Expectations Around Trust

Instilling trust organizationally begins with clarifying the behavior you expect of all employees. Several years ago, we introduced under the framework of our three core competencies (character, competence, and collaboration) a larger set of desired behaviors that apply to Kronites at all levels. We began basing 40 percent of employees' annual performance ratings on how well they adopted these behaviors. One behavior we emphasized was "establishing trust," which we defined as: "Gains the confidence and trust of others through principled leadership, sound business ethics, authenticity, and follow-through on commitments. Establishes open, candid, trusting relationships; treats all individuals fairly and with respect; maintains high standards of integrity."

In formulating this definition, we looked to behavior norms that had already existed to some extent in our organization, but that had never been identified and highlighted formally. Articulating organizational expectations around behavior is important. By defining trust, we established it as a key element of our culture. In addition, other behaviors and competencies we identified, such as "collaboration" and "open communication," also contributed to trust.

Deploy Tools to Help Your People Get to Know One Another Better

Like many companies, we have prospective hires complete a behavioral assessment—in our case, a tool called Predictive Index (PI)—that reveals traits such as how detail-oriented a person is, how extroverted, how patient, and so on. The results of this assessment allow us to increase the chances that personalities will mesh well within teams, which facilitates trust building as well as overall performance. After all, in team environments, understanding how your teammates operate allows you as either a manager or employee to set expectations properly and to avoid misunderstandings when others don't perform in expected ways. At Kronos, we train managers on how to use the tool and its results. Although PI doesn't single-handedly determine our hiring decisions, it does inform them, allowing us to develop probing questions around behaviors that we might not have otherwise considered.

I've found PI useful in my own capacity as a manager. Years ago, I managed an employee who was rather introverted and detail-oriented. Thanks to my exposure to PI, I knew that people with this personality type didn't require a lot of explanation when their managers assigned them tasks. Their PI suggested telling them to perform the task and leave it at that. If I as a manager delivered a more long-winded explanation, it would only frustrate them. At one point, when I was first beginning to use PI, I approached this employee and described how his personality differed from mine. To my surprise, he became emotional. "Aron, this is such a relief to me," he said. "It drives me crazy when you overexplain stuff to me. It's as if you don't trust me. I get it, just tell me what you want me to do." Because I understood this employee in a deeper way, we could avoid any misunderstanding that might have arisen due to our different needs and capacities. A higher level of trust could flourish.

Infuse the Principle of Trust into Your Policies

As I'll describe in Chapter 9, we revamped our time-off policies, doing away with fixed vacation time allocations and instead allowing open time off. Employees can decide when and how much time off they wish to take, so long as they discuss their plans with their managers, get their work done, and coordinate with them to minimize any disruptions to our business and to the service we provide to our customers. A number of considerations went into the framing of this policy, but one of them was our desire to show Kronites that we trusted them to get their work done and that we wouldn't look over their shoulders to dictate when they were in the office or on vacation. By showing trust in this way (we also show it through our longstanding openness to flexible, work-at-home arrangements), we further cement its importance within our culture.

Teach Managers to Nourish Trust in Their Teams

Manager training and accountability offer another important vehicle for trust building at the organizational level. I'll talk more about these subjects in the next chapter, but for now I'll note the emphasis we place on trust in our "Courage to Lead" manager training program (see figure on page 55). All of our hundreds of people managers attend this program, which instills trust and transparency by focusing managers on three key behavioral areas.

First, we ask managers to be both "bold" and "humble." In elaborating on these terms, we specifically ask managers to build trust by trusting people in their functional areas and beyond, and assuming that people are competent when tackling difficult issues. Don't jump to conclusions, and don't point fingers. Humbly accept that you don't have all the answers, boldly look to your people for insight and expertise, and ask questions that others dare not ask. We also instruct managers to share information openly and honestly and to make the tough decisions required to solve problems, additional expressions of boldness that will also help to build trusting relationships over time. One employee put it well: "As a manager, take responsibility when something is wrong. No excuses. Take ownership. Everything we do, we do together as a team. Good or bad." As we tell our managers, if they can't "be real" with employees, they simply won't gain their trust.

The second plank of our Courage to Lead model asks managers to "challenge and support" their team members. Managers should support team members—and build trust—by communicating a strategic vision (Chapter 5). Team members will gain confidence that their efforts at work meaningfully contribute to team and organizational goals. By empowering team members to innovate and take risks, managers further demonstrate the trust they place in their people. As one of our employees said of her manager, "I don't have to ask for permission. I feel comfortable enough to make a decision and my manager supports me." Another said: "My manager provides me independence and trusts me to do the right thing." Those are the kinds of responses we want from *everyone* who works at Kronos. Employees who feel trusted will return the favor, allowing a general atmosphere of trust to prevail. We also teach managers to build trust by creating an environment in which people can develop professionally and share their views. "Know where your employees want to go," one Kronite advised our managers. "Know their career path and set up a mentor or support system so that they can grow." If managers are challenging and supporting Kronites fully, Kronites will trust that managers have their best interests in mind as well as the team's.

The third plank of our Courage to Lead model instructs managers to "disrupt" their teams and the organizational status quo generally while also forging connections between team members. By challenging outdated norms and by helping team members forge connections across departments, managers inspire their team members' trust that they can remove organizational obstacles and facilitate their work. Likewise, by prioritizing customers and the company's interests, managers can help team members feel more confident in their motives and in the quality of their decision making.

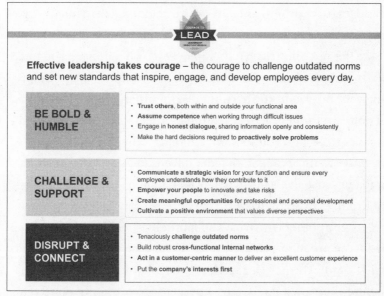

Effective leadership takes courage – the courage to challenge outdated norms and set new standards that inspire, engage, and develop employees every day.

BE BOLD & HUMBLE
- **Trust others**, both within and outside your functional area
- **Assume competence** when working through difficult issues
- Engage in **honest dialogue**, sharing information openly and consistently
- Make the hard decisions required to **proactively solve problems**

CHALLENGE & SUPPORT
- **Communicate a strategic vision** for your function and ensure every employee understands how they contribute to it
- **Empower your people** to innovate and take risks
- **Create meaningful opportunities** for professional and personal development
- **Cultivate a positive environment** that values diverse perspectives

DISRUPT & CONNECT
- Tenaciously **challenge outdated norms**
- Build robust **cross-functional internal networks**
- **Act in a customer-centric manner** to deliver an excellent customer experience
- Put the **company's interests first**

Courage to Lead model

We train managers across these behavioral areas in a variety of ways, depending on the amount of time they've spent in their role. New managers receive basic training that defines our expectations around them. Four to six months into their new roles, managers undergo an intensive, two-day training in which they practice Courage to Lead behaviors in the context of specific situations and challenges. As we discover behavioral weaknesses in managers, we give them extra training in the form of half-day modules. We also support them with one-on-one coaching as needed.

Throughout this training, we practice what we preach when it comes to open communications. We don't minimize the difficulty managers will have when it comes to trusting employees. Trust is hard, especially if you haven't lived or worked in an open and supportive environment, or if you have an anxious or controlling personality. That's where the courage part of Courage to Lead features prominently. We ask our managers to muster up a resolve that in many cases might be unfamiliar and even scary. Take the risk and trust your employees. As a manager, you must learn to feel comfortable both with uncertainty and with having your boss hold you accountable for other people's decisions. If you can't imagine ever feeling comfortable, then you won't inspire trust, and you shouldn't manage others.

All of our people managers have undergone this training, and our trust levels have increased palpably. In 2017, 88 percent of Kronites in an internal survey agreed that "At Kronos, people treat one another with trust and mutual respect," up three points from the previous year. A full 82 percent of respondents agreed with "I trust the people I work with to put the work group's goals before their own goals," up 3 percent from the previous year. Likewise, in 2017, 93 percent of 1,335 Kronites polled for the Great Place to Work's Trust Index survey in the United States indicated our company was a great place to work, while 93 percent reported that our "management is honest and ethical in its business practices," and 92 percent "trusted in management's competence at running the business."[1] Whereas previously some Kronos managers might have learned about trust by virtue of their direct interaction with me and others in the company who practiced it, we've now established trust as a baseline expectation throughout our organization. Managers beware: at Kronos, you *will* be held accountable for trusting behavior. I suggest you require the same in your organization.

Pursue the Other Principles Described in This Book

Other chapters in this book present an array of organizational practices and policies that help establish norms of trust in various respects. For instance, because we take care to communicate transparently, honestly, and frequently, Kronites are far more inclined to trust their bosses at all levels. Our efforts to take care of Kronites (Chapter 7) and keep them safe (Chapter 8) establish our workplaces as spaces where employees can trust one another to look out for them and treat them respectfully. The work we put into framing, communicating, and resourcing our strategies (Chapter 5) allows Kronites to trust their leaders and feel confident that leaders are making effective decisions. And our efforts to welcome Kronites from different cultures and geographies (Chapter 12) help employees trust that they will be accepted and their perspectives valued.

FAIL SOONER

If it's possible for individuals and organizations to enhance trust, is it really worth the effort? Or, in this rough-and-tumble world of ours, would it behoove companies to set aside this "soft stuff" and focus on something more tangible, like designing amazing products?

Based on our experience at Kronos, focusing a team or an organization on trust is absolutely worth it. Since I've become CEO, we've grown our revenues from around $500 million in 2005 to more than $1.4 billion in 2018 . . . and we're still growing. Obviously, results like that owe to many factors, but I strongly believe that our culture of trust has proven fundamental. It would be nice if we could quantitatively track the incidence of trusting behaviors throughout Kronos and then demonstrate statistical correlations with measures like engagement, retention, market share, and revenues. But I don't need statistics to convince me. As so many Kronites will affirm, both the spread of trusting relationships throughout Kronos and their pivotal role in our growth story are obvious.

I've suggested why trust might contribute to higher engagement and retention, but let's quickly consider a couple of specific ways that it helps drive business results. In 2009, we assigned Chris, the executive I introduced earlier, to assemble a team that would create, sell, and manage our first cloud software offerings. Chris did a fantastic job, as I knew he would, launching the initiative and bringing in an annualized $40 million of revenue by 2012. By the fall of 2012, however, the business was faltering. A variety of performance issues had cropped up, including data center mishaps, customer outages, even some natural disasters that impeded our delivery of services. Customers were getting angry, and sales reps began grumbling about feeling unsupported.

Chris did his best to resolve these problems. But as the months went by, we made little headway and had to confront a difficult truth: he was out of his depth. As skilled and experienced as he was, he had never managed a data center before, or handled other specialized parts of that business.

One morning in December 2012, Chris knocked on my office door and asked if we could chat. "Aron," he said, "I'm sorry about the problems we're having with the cloud, but I'm not your guy to fix this. I just don't know how to do it." He might have expected a stern lecture from me, or some kind of "punishment" for having failed. But I only cared about one thing: If Chris couldn't fix this business, who could? How could we devise an alternative solution so that we could ultimately succeed at being a cloud company?

It took us a few weeks to figure out a way forward, but we wound up recruiting another leader within Kronos to take over the team. This new leader helped us solve our service issues so that we could stabilize and grow the business. Today, our cloud offerings bring in more than $400 million in revenues, accounting for over 90 percent of our new customer accounts. Customers are incredibly happy and are served by a world-class cloud operations team.

Chris didn't have to approach me right away. He could have struggled with this part of the business for another year or two, hiding or explaining away the failures as best he could. Had he feared my response, he might have done exactly that. Instead, Chris came to me immediately because he knew that I trusted him and that I would react in a healthy, rational, respectful way, even when confronted by unwelcome news. This mutual trust enabled us to confront the problem head-on, devising a sensible solution together. Our conversations and the decisions we made enabled us to come up with solutions for our cloud operations that were much more profitable and sustainable.

MY SECRET WEAPON: TRUST

If you haven't trusted others easily in the past, now is the time to start. If you have, then rededicate yourself to deepening your trusting relationships. Look around: Are you empowering team members by encouraging their creativity and autonomy, or are you inadvertently stifling them? Are you communicating as openly and honestly as you think, setting an example for others?

And are your expectations about trust-promoting behavior as clearly defined as possible?

Despite the effort it requires, trusting others still represents a far easier way to manage. Think of what happens when you learn to let go of fear, anxiety, and control. All that effort you expended worrying about how one of your people would perform, all that time and energy you spent monitoring progress, now can go toward other pursuits that truly add value, like spending more time ideating, collaborating, and innovating. Trusting others doesn't only yield greater engagement directly by inspiring loyalty and affection and by contributing to others' growth and advancement. It supports engagement indirectly by freeing you up to take a variety of other actions that build personal relationships and drive growth. People often wonder how I manage to respond so quickly to every employee e-mail, and how I have so many in-person conversations with Kronites, while also fulfilling the "ordinary" duties of a CEO.

Now you know. Trust.

4

Hold Managers Accountable

One fundamental belief I've cultivated during my tenure at Kronos is that every employee deserves a great manager. Managers are integral to employee engagement and overall job satisfaction. The best, most talented people would rather have a bad job working for a great manager than a great job working for a bad manager. As I mentioned earlier, employees might join organizations because of the company and the compensation package, but they *leave* organizations because of their manager. Gallup even found, as a *Harvard Business Review* article noted, that "half of all employees in the United States have quit jobs at some point in their careers in order to get away from their bosses."[1] That's scandalous!

How do you improve the quality of your managers? The standard answer is training—lots of it. Most large companies offer some kind of training program for their managers, as do we. But training alone isn't cutting it. A 2015 survey of 1,000 employees in the United States found widespread dissatisfaction with bosses, with a majority of respondents faulting ineffective leaders for "not recognizing employee achievements," "not giving clear directions," "not having time to meet with employees," and "refusing to talk to subordinates."[2] What managers need, in addition to training, is accountability, including performance metrics and benchmarking. Otherwise, their efforts will diminish over time, and any formal training they receive will do little good. In the words of one Kronite, managing people and focusing on their development is "always the first thing that falls off the plate when you're prioritizing things."

For most of our history, we lacked quantitative metrics that specifically tracked manager performance. After I became CEO, that started to bug me. I couldn't understand why almost all engagement measures traditionally deployed by organizations focused on the employee-company relationship. Organizations asked employees how happy they were with compensation, communications, training, and the like, while failing to probe the employee-*manager* relationship. Didn't organizations want to know whether managers were serving employees well, providing clear direction, career guidance, helpful feedback, and other kinds of support? Didn't they want to know if managers were building trusting relationships grounded in open and honest communication?

FROM CULTIVATING MANAGERS TO MEASURING THEM

For the first decade of my tenure as CEO, these questions remained just that—questions. We had other priorities to address to become a great place to work. As I've recounted, our early attempts to improve our culture included hiring a seasoned chief people officer and defining culture as a strategic priority. We also began paying closer attention to employee responses on our annual engagement survey, which we'd had in place since 2005. We had developed a reputation for not acting on feedback from the survey, with employees asking, "Why should I participate in these surveys when no action is taken?" We started to take action based on employee feedback. In addition, we began holding managers accountable for telling us what they were doing to improve engagement, checking on their progress in subsequent surveys. I also began to trigger change simply by practicing many of the leadership behaviors described in this book. By 2013, we had made significant strides in becoming a great place to work. In 2010, 61 percent of Kronites felt engaged. By 2013, thanks to our initial attempts to improve our culture, 73 percent did (and today, of course, our engagement numbers are much higher).

We had by this time been undertaking a dramatic transformation of our business model, moving our products into the cloud and selling them to customers as a subscription service. By 2013, we realized that despite the efforts we'd made to improve our culture, we had much more work to do. Becoming a software-as-a-service (SaaS) company was taxing our workforce as never before. Consultants we'd hired identified a range of specific manager and employee behaviors that typically allow SaaS companies to succeed. In addition to having everyone work harder and longer than they had been, we'd need Kronites to become more disciplined, collaborative, communicative, and daring. We'd also require more flexibility. Some employees would see key dimensions of their job change, while others might have to find employment elsewhere. How would we undertake these dramatic changes without compromising the important cultural gains we'd already made? How could we apply pressure to our workforce without employee engagement, retention, and other measures plummeting?

To maintain the affection, commitment, and loyalty of employees, and to retain our attractiveness to potential recruits, we took two primary courses of action. First, we reconfigured our employee benefits—a process I'll describe in Chapter 9. Second, we intensified our efforts to grow our culture, mobilizing our managers as part of the effort. In 2013, we highlighted the strategic importance of employees by defining and branding our culture, calling it *WorkInspired*. The name reflected our understanding of the employment partnership: Kronos agreed to provide an inspiring place to work, and in exchange we asked that Kronites perform their work tasks in an inspired way. To further enhance our culture, we altered how we measured employee performance, emphasizing three core behavioral competencies: character, competence, and collaboration. We affirmed that we cared not only about our performance itself, but about *how* employees achieved their results. Recognizing the key role that managers play, we created Building Management Capabilities, a training course for all managers that guides them through effective coaching, development planning, performance evaluation, and other managerial core competencies.

In 2015, we launched Courage to Lead as a one-time training course, setting out a three-part behavioral model for all Kronos managers. This model sought to describe both the organization we were at the time and the organization we aspired to be even more fully going forward. As I described in Chapter 3, we asked managers to be bold yet humble, to challenge Kronites but also support them, and to disrupt existing practices but also make efforts to engage and connect with people. Behaviors we associated with these three planks included trusting others, assuming their competence, communicating openly and honestly, and making hard decisions to aggressively solve problems throughout the organization.

Subsequently, we created a system of ongoing training around Courage to Lead that continues to evolve. Prior to becoming managers, high-performing individuals who think they might want to lead teams can take a self-led course called Courage to Lead: Emerging Leaders that exposes them to our expectations of managers, and that allows them to compare their current skills and behaviors with what we require in our Courage to Lead model. They can then discuss any skills gap with their manager, taking steps to build their skills in advance of becoming managers themselves. Once employees become managers, they undergo Courage to Lead: Jumpstart, a self-led assimilation program for new managers that outlines the key responsibilities of the role, the Courage to Lead model, competencies and goals, and the key processes and programs in place to support them. A few months later, new managers can take a two-day skill-building course called Courage to Lead: Foundations during which we confront them with specific situations and challenges so that they can practice applying the Courage to Lead model.

At about the time we rolled out Courage to Lead, we also instituted a campaign called Make the 5HIFT that was designed to instill five specific behaviors we'd need to thrive as a SaaS company. As Lisa, who headed up our Transformation Management Office (TMO), a group we created to lead our organizational change, recalls, "We were asking people to act very differently and to do things very differently. They needed to enthusiastically adopt that we were transforming our entire business, and that we would have a new SaaS-centric culture."[3] Make the 5HIFT focused on the five behavioral areas that we identified as gaps for us: "customer first, humility, empowerment, collaboration, and courage." We also identified specific behaviors to eliminate, including pushing all big decisions up to the executive committee, finger-pointing, pushing client problems off to other teams within Kronos, siloed thinking, the excessive tailoring of offerings to individual customers, and so on. Make the 5HIFT sought to influence employees to demonstrate desired SaaS behaviors as well as to understand that they all had to step up and help us become a SaaS company.

Together, Make the 5HIFT and Courage to Lead deepened our commitment to a culture based on trust, transparency, and other values described in this book. But we still lacked that key element: manager measurement and accountability. In 2016, we finally took this next step. I had wanted to field a short and simple survey to measure managers' performance, asking Kronites blunt questions about their managers like "If you could decide today whether to work for your current manager or not, would you?" At a conference I attended, one of the speakers, the head of human resources for a large global company, described how his company had jettisoned annual performance reviews. Instead, the company asked managers to rate employees every quarter, filling out an online survey that asked, "If you had the choice to hire this employee again, would you?" I loved the boldness of that, but I didn't get why this company would only have managers ask this question about their team members. Why not also ask employees whether they'd work for their manager again?

Our chief people officer convinced me that we should take a more thoughtful and sophisticated route, so that we could understand *why* people did or didn't like their managers. Building off of our Courage to Lead model, we researched the behavior of outstanding managers, contacting other companies for their perspective, studying the specific practices employed by top Kronos managers, and querying a group of Kronites about actions they associated with excellent managers. Compiling all of this research, we created a concise profile of a great Kronos manager, refining it in employee focus groups to build a new model focused on the manager-employee relationship. Under this model, managers were expected to communicate openly and honestly with their teams, sharing information and providing constant feedback. They were expected to empower and enable their team members, encouraging judicious risk-taking and trusting employees. They were expected to develop and encourage their team members, fostering excellence and providing support and coaching. And they were expected to support the whole employee, honoring work-life balance and appreciating the diverse strengths that employees bring to bear.

With this work in hand, we reviewed our existing employee engagement survey questions to determine whether or to what extent they measured these behaviors. We had posed dozens of questions as part of our engagement survey, covering areas like business strategy and process, talent strategy and process, our culture, and impressions about senior leadership. We modified certain questions and added others that focused specifically on the managerial behaviors we'd identified. Out of this work, we created the Manager Effectiveness Index, or MEI, which captured employee judgments about managers' performance.

LAUNCHING MEI

We administered the manager effectiveness questions to Kronites as part of the engagement survey we executed twice each year. Employees responded on a five-point scale, with responses ranging from "strongly agree" to "strongly disagree."

My Manager—Communicate

1. My manager is available when I need him/her.
2. My manager makes an effort to get the opinions and thinking of the people in our work group.
3. My manager regularly shares relevant information from his/her manager and functional leadership.
4. My manager ensures I understand the business strategy and how my work influences it.
5. My manager provides ongoing feedback that helps me improve my performance.
6. My manager communicates clear performance goals for me.
7. My manager helps me understand my compensation and conveys the rationale for pay decisions.
8. Within the last six months, my manager had a productive discussion with me/our team about his/her plans to address the feedback from the Manager Effectiveness Index.

My Manager—Develop

9. My manager challenges our work group to meet higher standards of performance.
10. My manager actively looks for opportunities for me to grow and improve my skills.
11. My manager has had a meaningful discussion with me about my career development in the past six months.
12. My manager has ongoing, meaningful discussions with me about my professional development.

My Manager—Empower

13. My manager empowers me to make decisions that enable me to do my job effectively.

14. My manager helps me navigate barriers and roadblocks that prevent me from working effectively.
15. My manager encourages our work group to take appropriate risks to improve business results.

My Manager—Support

16. My manager does what he/she can to ensure I have the flexibility to balance my work and personal life.
17. My manager truly cares about me as an employee.
18. My manager shows appreciation when I do a good job.
19. My manager provides the right amount of direction.

We didn't just throw MEI out there, leaving managers to make sense of it on their own. First, we only shared the initial batch of MEI scores with the manager being evaluated, not his or her manager. This would give managers time to digest their scores and think about forming a personal action plan. (Starting with the second round of scores, we shared results with managers and their managers.) Second, to protect anonymity, we only shared employee MEI feedback with managers who had three or more direct reports respond to the questions. Third, since we expected these managers to use the feedback to create and implement development plans for themselves, we provided them with materials that helped them understand MEI's format and purpose, interpret the data, and identify areas for improvement. Fourth, we gave managers access to one-on-one coaching and a set of training materials to help them hone their skills. These training programs spelled out a range of possible actions managers could take to develop specific skills in which they might have shown weakness. The training also helped managers discuss their evaluation results with team members, giving them sample agendas for conversation and suggesting ways that they might frame key ideas. We regarded these discussions as critical to fostering trust and open communication between employees and managers and to reinforcing accountability.

When we first announced MEI, we tried to present it in a way that wouldn't put people managers on the defensive. We explained our philosophy that every employee deserves a great manager, as well as how important we believed managers to be to employees' experience. As we told managers, our intention was to give them a tool that would help them improve. Although most managers appreciated the tool, some perceived our entire effort as excessive. "You're putting yet another item on my plate?" managers said. "It's enough that I have to manage my people every day and do performance reviews. Oh, and I have to undergo Courage to Lead training. Now you're telling me that I have to care about my MEI scores, too? It's too much!" We had to absorb this pushback and work with it as best we could. As our chief people officer said, "We were moving from a company that wasn't as sophisticated about management to one that was. That's not going to happen by itself. There will be some portion of the population that kicks and screams."

WORKING WITH MEI

Fortunately, the number of naysayers was relatively small. Since our first round of MEI scores, we've seen an ethic of continuous improvement take root among our managers. "I don't know that I ever thought this," said Becky, one of our managers, "but I'll just spill it: it's not easy to be a good manager. Even for the best managers, you still have to work at it every day." In some cases, MEI results alerted managers to weaknesses they didn't even know they had—they didn't communicate well, for instance, or they didn't spend enough time helping employees strategize about their career aspirations. These managers addressed their weak areas, and in many cases improved their scores (68 percent of our lowest-scoring managers improved within the first year). Our formerly mediocre or average managers were becoming *great* managers! As for the weakest managers who couldn't improve, even with the intensive coaching and training we gave them, most have either left the company or given up managerial roles.

One of our leaders, whom I'll call Carly, hadn't had many "career talks" with her direct reports, and was amazed at what happened when she finally did. She learned so much by asking questions such as, "What are your career aspirations?" and "What would you like to be doing in three or five years?" To her surprise, some of her direct reports desired a more aggressive career track, while others who were new parents wanted time to figure out how to balance their careers with their family obligations. Based on Carly's conversations, which were prompted by our MEI, she improved connections she had with those individuals and was better able to plan for her team's growth and evolution.

Adam, one of our leaders, learned from MEI that he wasn't having enough conversations with employees two levels down who reported to managers he was supervising. These lower-level employees wanted a chance to communicate their concerns directly with a leader in their department. "I have to be conscious that it's important," Adam said, "and all of our schedules are crazy sometimes, but you have to make the time to ensure that employees are engaged, and if they're not feeling engagement from their own direct manager, then they have face time with me." For Adam, MEI's underlying value lay in its ability to foster honest communication and responsibility. "I'm not going to hide from [a subpar score]. It's an area that needs to be improved. Let's talk through it. Let's figure it out. Let's be a better group together."

Some managers got creative in using the results. Interested in improving his scores, one manager—I'll call him Ben—decided he wanted deeper feedback from members of his team. He knew that if he asked team members about his performance individually, they might feel reluctant to speak frankly. So he brought them all together in a conference room and then left, asking them collectively to leave detailed comments about his performance. When he returned, he'd have a list of anonymous comments that he could use to modify his behavior and approach. As his manager related, "He was able to use that tool in a nonthreatening manner to get the exact feedback and examples [he needed]. It's been so much fun to see his scores improve over the last 18 months." Another manager followed up on her MEI scores by having each of her team members write a report that captured their feelings about their development and plotted out a plan for helping them feel even more engaged. Afterward, she met with each Kronite to review and discuss the plan. As one of her employees noted, "It was a nice add-on to our normal, one-on-one interactions."

MEI has sometimes prompted managers to work together to improve. A healthy rivalry has cropped up between our sales and professional services organizations as to who can get the most employees to complete the survey. "We turned it into a competition," a Kronite leader in our services group said. "I don't care how high or low [our return rate] is, as long as it's higher than our sales department's!" Her colleague on our sales team concurred. "If we're going to be competitive on something, let it be engagement! It's a big deal here." As these and other managers have also noticed, MEI has tended to free employees to make more suggestions for process improvement. Because conversations about manager performance are now much more common, employees feel empowered to speak up. "My team feels like it has a voice now," one manager said, pointing to the many suggestions her team members have made.

All of this effort on the part of managers to improve what they do gets me *really* excited. From my own career, I know first-hand how easy it is to make mistakes as a manager, and how much learning is required to manage others well. I also know how rewarding it is when you do improve and become more competent.

Back when I was a young manager in my twenties, I worked nonstop, putting in as much as 80 or 90 hours a week. I didn't have a family yet—Kronos was my life. Because I worked so hard, I used to expect people on my team to do the same. When they didn't, I became frustrated. One day, I complained to a particular team member that he wasn't working hard enough. "Aron," he said, "I'm not you. I don't want to work as hard as you work." His tone was firm, but not aggressive or mean. That conversation taught me how important it was for managers to listen to people and respect their needs. If I was going to continue to crack the whip, my team members probably wouldn't show me much loyalty, and their impression of the company would suffer, too. If I wanted to build a strong, committed team, I would need to treat people more respectfully, paying closer attention to *their* needs and desires. I would have to do all I could to facilitate and inspire their creativity, so that they could do their best, most innovative work.

I happened to learn this lesson because a particular team member was strong enough to speak up. I wonder how much more quickly I would have learned it if I had a tool like MEI at my disposal to help bring my weaker skills to the surface. How long had I been driving people harder than what was productive? How much better would my team have been performing all along had I been more sensitive to their needs?

Above and beyond the improvement it spurs, MEI delivers an array of other benefits to our organization. For one, it helps attract both recruits and customers to our brand. Our human resources team has begun to use MEI as a selling point to job candidates, helping introduce them to our company culture and its focus on individual improvement and managerial account-ability. As human resources team members tell recruits, Kronos feels so strongly about the relationship between managers and employees that the company polls employees twice a year to hear how they feel about it. Given the horror stories people tell about bad managers, who wouldn't want to work at a company like this?

I've also used MEI to communicate the uniqueness of our culture to customers. Customers sometimes seem puzzled at first, wondering why I'd want to talk with them about our man-agers, much less metrics relating to our managers. As I explain, Kronos sees itself as an ethical company that treats its employees well, and that means building strong managers, which *in turn* means holding managers accountable. I put the question back to them: if you're not asking your other vendors about managers and employee engagement, maybe you should. Do you want to do business with someone who treats employees poorly? What kind of experience could you hope to receive from those poorly treated employees?

A GREAT JOB *AND* A GREAT MANAGER

To date, MEI's impact on our culture has been astounding. In 2016, 81 percent of employees rated their managers with a "strongly agree" or "agree" on the MEI questions. In 2017, 87 percent of employees rated their managers favorably. In 2016, 78 percent of Kronites rated their managers favorably for the performance feedback they delivered; in 2017, 86 percent did. In 2016, 85 percent of Kronites said their managers truly cared about them as an employee. In 2017, that number was 90 percent. Improvements such as these have gone hand in hand with jumps in employee engagement. During our first year of using this tool in conjunction with our preexisting manager training programs, our employee engagement score rose from 84 out of 100, where it had been stuck for three years, to an 87. Our retention metric (asking the question, "Would you consider leaving Kronos in the next year?") is now an amazing 88 percent saying no. Our voluntary turnover of strong performers declined by 1 percent, saving us at least $1 million in expenses. Was MEI a good value for our organization? I think so!

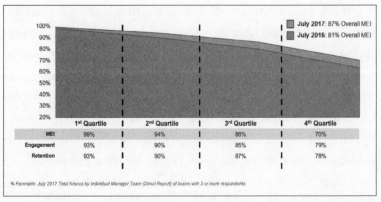

	1st Quartile	2nd Quartile	3rd Quartile	4th Quartile
MEI	99%	94%	86%	70%
Engagement	93%	90%	85%	79%
Retention	93%	90%	87%	78%

July 2017: 87% Overall MEI
July 2016: 81% Overall MEI

% Favorable: July 2017 Total Kronos by Individual Manager Team (Direct Report) of teams with 3 or more respondents.

MEI Results by Quartile Showing Correlation Between
Manager Effectiveness with Engagement and Retention

Our MEI tool was admittedly a bit of an experiment. We suspected it would make a difference but weren't sure. Now that we've had multiple rounds of scores, analyzing our data with the help of scientists at the University of South Carolina's Darla Moore School of Business, we have established a clear statistical relationship between strong manager behavior and employee engagement.

MEI isn't perfect. For instance, if a manager with just four direct reports is addressing employee performance issues, even one person who responds negatively will drag down the manager's overall MEI score. Still, MEI explains a great deal of the variability between highly engaged employees and their less engaged counterparts. Employees with managers in the lowest 25 percent of MEI scores have engagement scores 13 points lower than those with managers in the highest MEI quartile. Their retention levels are also 14 points lower. It isn't a difference in pay or work conditions that matters most when it comes to engagement—it's the relationship between employees and their managers.

If you want employees to love where they work, you can't just focus on them and how they feel. You have to train and coach managers, and you have to hold them accountable. The broader goal, as I've suggested, isn't just to help individual managers, but to create a climate of continuous improvement. We've observed a ripple effect regarding manager effectiveness, whereby managers' MEI scores correlate with those of their direct-report managers. Great managers model behaviors that directly impact how their people manage their own teams. While this mentor-type impact often happens organically, the MEI program amplifies this effect by triggering open, honest, and very pointed conversations about leadership style. As some managers work on improving their skills, the performance of other managers below them improves, too.

With workloads as strenuous as they already are, it's not easy to get a cadre of managers to work aggressively on their skills. But it's possible. A few years ago, we had managers say to us, "Wait, I know my business card says 'manager,' but you want me to actually *manage* people?" We don't get that anymore. Instead, we see managers across Kronos providing sustained, focused, and individually tailored mentorship to their reports. And our entire company has reaped considerable benefit. People might run from bosses they hate, but take it from us, the converse is also true. If you combine a great job with a great manager, you've hit the jackpot. Morale improves. People engage. Anything becomes possible.

5

Get Serious About Strategy

During the summer of 2017, I got into a disagreement with Steve, a leader on our marketing team, over how best to communicate our corporate strategy to employees. In our attempts to build engagement and develop our culture, we had started to brand our strategy, associating it with a slogan or "wrapper" to make it easy to understand and remember. For the past several years, that wrapper, originally conceived by Steve, had been "Kronos 5.0," a reference to our reinvention as a cloud company, the fifth major transformation in our 40-year history. This moniker in turn contained three pillars: Customer, Cloud, and Company. Our Kronos 5.0 strategy was to continue to delight our customers, mobilizing our deep knowledge about their industries. It was to continue our efforts to become a great organization, a powerhouse of growth and innovation as well as a "great place to work." And it was to continue to become a great cloud company, developing ongoing relationships with our cloud customers and transforming how we operated internally to maximize the value we delivered as a cloud company.

The Kronos 5.0 wrapper had generated excitement and mobilized employees, helping us to reach and even exceed our goals. Between 2014 and 2017, 90 percent of new customers bought Kronos software as a service in the cloud. We had anticipated a temporary revenue dip as we transitioned to a subscription-based business model. Subscription revenues flow in on a monthly basis, as opposed to all at once under an on-premise licensing model. Over the short term, we would see less revenue, but over a longer time period, as those monthly fees kept accruing, we expected significantly higher overall revenues. To our surprise and delight, the short-term revenue dip never occurred because Kronites everywhere pulled together, helping us to increase sales more than anticipated. Explaining the benefits of our new model, they convinced many of our existing customers, whose existing license-based software we maintained, to begin using our subscription services. That, in turn, delivered more value to the company. The Kronos 5.0 branding hadn't single-handedly produced that result, but it had certainly helped by clarifying our strategy and focusing Kronites on its execution.

By the summer of 2017, though, I felt that Kronos 5.0 had become stale. In a few months, we would announce the single most important new product in Kronos's history, and it seemed odd to accompany that announcement with our existing strategic language. I wanted to rally Kronites, pump them up to take us to even greater heights. Kronos 5.0 just wouldn't help me do that. It might strike Kronites as "old news," not particularly engaging or inspiring any longer, and at odds with our exciting new product. Or at least, that's what I thought. Our marketing leader Steve passionately disagreed. He felt Kronos 5.0 remained quite viable, as broadly speaking, we had yet to complete the company's fifth reinvention. It would seem awkward, he thought, to introduce a new slogan for what was essentially a continuation of our ongoing strategy.

I heard Steve out—I really did. In my experience, a willingness to challenge one's boss and stand by one's beliefs often marks a truly engaged employee, so I very much appreciated his arguments. Still, none of them persuaded me. I knew that evangelizing the message starts at the top, and that if I wasn't feeling it, it wouldn't come across as authentic when I communicated with employees. So, at the end of our meeting, I made a decision. We would have a new strategy wrapper this year. And it would once again fall on Steve to create it.

A few weeks later, I introduced Kronites attending our annual sales kickoff event to our revolutionary new product, Workforce Dimensions, a workforce management software suite delivered in the cloud that automates critical workforce processes such as timekeeping, scheduling, and leave management. At the same time, I rolled out "UP," a new wrapper that connected Kronites to our strategy (see figure on page 82). As I explained to the audience, "UP" stood for "Unlimited Potential." Although our company had already achieved incredible results, Workforce Dimensions presented us with an unprecedented growth opportunity. In the years ahead, we'd innovate like never before, increase our sales, and reach new heights in revenue and profitability. Individual Kronites would also have a chance to move UP, taking their careers to new heights. Under UP, we'd focus on seven strategic areas: offering great products, serving customers as a cloud company, boosting innovation, making our products "global ready" (in other words, deployable in all countries), running an efficient company, putting customers first, and continuing to work hard to be a great place to work. On the back of this strategy, we only had one direction in which to move: UP. And the way we would do it is by leveraging "us"—the remarkable talent Kronos had in every corner of our business. As I told Kronites, a brighter future was "UP to us." It was up to us to capitalize on the opportunities we saw on the horizon.

Our Unlimited Potential (UP) strategy

Now, you might wonder why I as the CEO cared so much about an internal marketing slogan. Did it really matter how we rallied Kronites around our strategy? Didn't the CEO have more important business matters to worry about? And why would I mention our slogans here, in a book about employee engagement?

Many leaders and managers underestimate the links between strategy and creating a workplace that employees love. Indeed, many underestimate the role of strategy in general. Leaders and managers sometimes say, "I hope this works out." But as an old saying goes, hope is not a strategy—not when it comes to achieving organizational goals of any kind, and certainly not when it comes to building an engaged workforce and a flourishing organization. In general, people feel happier and more confident working in organizations and teams with a clear sense of direction, and their jobs seem more meaningful if they understand what the company is trying to accomplish and, in turn, how they personally contribute to the company's success. People also feel more comfortable placing their trust in leaders who are setting a clear direction, making sound decisions, and moving the organization ahead. That trust in turn leads to greater engagement. As one Kronite told us, "I have every confidence in our senior management team. I truly believe our executives make the right decisions when it comes to keeping our business thriving and moving forward." This employee listed his confidence in leadership as a "compelling reason" for why he has stayed at Kronos.

Some of the smartest, most talented employees keep close tabs on companies' strategies, factoring this into their decision to join organizations or remain within them. One Kronite who returned to our company after a period at another organization cited our strategy as a prime reason for his return. "I kept following the company closely when I was out," he said, "and knew how strong the Kronos leadership team [was], as well as its commitment to the company's continuous success and growth. I was truly impressed when Kronos crossed the $1 billion mark, knew about [Kronos's acquisition of other companies], [its] global expansion and the impressive investments made by Kronos investors." If we hadn't attended to our strategy as closely as we do, perhaps this employee would not have felt comfortable rejoining, or felt as engaged and enthusiastic ever since.

If you're a manager in the middle of the organization, you might wonder whether you should really focus so much on strategy. The answer is that at every level of an organization, an individual's work only has meaning if it flows organically out of a broader strategy, geared toward achieving an inspiring collective goal. Managers can devise local strategies that their teams or departments can use to deliver on the broader company strategy.

And they can help ensure that all employees understand the strategy and its connection to their work.

No matter how many people you lead or manage, if you want them to feel passionate about their work, you simply must attend to strategy. In particular, you must perform three distinct tasks well: devise a strategy, resource the strategy, and evangelize the strategy. How? Let's take a look at each of these activities, and examine how we at Kronos have approached them.

DEVISE A STRATEGY

At Kronos, we've long framed our strategies on an annual basis, doing so through a series of informal conversations among senior leaders. When I became CEO, I decided to make our corporate planning much more rigorous, data-driven, and inclusive than ever before. Today, after a number of tweaks and updates, our self-designed process has matured into a real point of pride for our organization, with deliberations that are much more comprehensive, systematic, and serious—as far as I can tell—than at many other companies.

It takes us four to five months each year to "work the strategy" for the upcoming year. Starting in February, an external facilitator interviews me, other members of my leadership team, and five to 10 additional leaders within Kronos from areas such as product development, sales, services, marketing, and strategy to identify our strategic priorities and areas of interest. We purposely select individuals with an eye toward accessing diverse ideas and viewpoints. On the basis of these interviews, we decide on a small number of key themes that we'll discuss during a three-day strategy off-site. We'll then spend a number of weeks collecting data relevant to the strategic questions and briefing all participants on the topics we plan to cover. This data collection can be quite extensive, involving multiple departments within Kronos and including market, survey, and financial data. The strategy session typically takes place in May and results in a list of initiatives and guidelines for their implementation. A few months later, we meet again to refine this list before proceeding to the next phase, creating budgets around our strategic priorities.

All told, our strategy process spans hundreds of hours of conversation, which are built in turn on hundreds of additional hours of research and analysis, all before our formal meetings take place. As CEO, my role is to push for hard data wherever it's available (something I do in all meetings I attend where decisions are made, not just strategy meetings). What will we lose by reducing resources on a project? Why should we target a new industry? How much money will we save by altering our vacation policy? It's more work to collect and analyze data, and some people in our organization chafe against it. "Aron, you drive us crazy sometimes," they say. "You just want so much data, so much detail, before you make a decision." Yes, I do, because that kind of intellectual curiosity pays off. We need data—lots of it—in order to make better, more thoughtful decisions.

My goal throughout our strategy process is to assure that we understand the truth of our business. If an existing strategy or tactic isn't working, we need to know that so we can change course. In 2017, we scrutinized our existing strategy of growing revenues by rapidly expanding our operations into new global markets. We determined it wasn't working. We were operating in a number of countries but were finding it too hard to achieve meaningful business results. We hadn't been losing money— we simply hadn't realized sizable profits in specific countries. It was time to take stock. What did the numbers say? As it turned out, they confirmed our suspicions about our global operations and led to a collective conviction that we needed to change course. We decided to keep our existing operations in place but scale back our plans for future expansion, all along continuing to target customers in markets around the world, just as we had been (we didn't need to establish physical offices in specific countries to cultivate multinational accounts). If we had stayed with our existing strategy, we would have continued to deploy our resources inefficiently, quite possibly for years. Because we pushed ourselves to ask the tough questions, we could change direction more quickly and deploy resources where they really could generate big returns for us.

Every leader and manager must do his or her best to expose reality. It's so important—not just for strategy, but for the everyday running of a business. Every decision you make, however small, should rest on an abiding concern for the truth of the matter, and you should go to great lengths to obtain actual data rather than merely estimating it or relying on gut instinct. When we were considering whether to relocate our headquarters, some people raised concerns that the walk from the parking lot at the new building was too far. Our leader in charge of the project could have dismissed these concerns, saying, "It doesn't seem too far." Instead, he went to the new building, parked as far away as he could, and timed himself as he walked to the building. It took him exactly five minutes. Now he could go back to the Kronites who had raised concerns with hard evidence backing up his judgment. This is a trivial example, but that's the point: day-to-day, exposing reality means making that extra effort to know the facts.

If you don't take a hard look at reality, trouble will likely follow. At a meeting of a company I advise, one executive grimly warned that the company had a problem: it had lost six of its top leaders. "We have to do something," this executive said. "They are leaving because they're not getting paid enough. We have to hand out more stock options to make us a more attractive employer." I later asked the CEO to show me data about turnover. It turned out that only three executives had left, not six. In their exit interviews, these departing employees related that their decisions had little to do with money, but instead reflected lifestyle considerations, like their desire for a reduced workload. With the data in hand, it was clear: the executive's interpretation of the problem had been incorrect. Instead of handing out more stock options, the company would have done better attending to job satisfaction. If employees see leadership make enough decisions that are at odds with reality, their trust plummets, and their engagement, too.

When it comes to strategy, it's important that participants at our off-site retreat arrive each year having already reviewed the data. That way, we can spend our time working through the substantive issues rather than passively watching PowerPoint presentations. And by "working through" the issues, I mean arguing. These strategy sessions aren't occasions for rubber-stamping decisions that I as the CEO have already made. We do the work of deliberating together. I don't possess a monopoly on good ideas. We really need a frank, spirited exchange of views to arrive at innovative, optimum results. Everyone present must have a say, which is why I'll frequently go around the room to ask people for their contributions and insights.

Because we have the collective courage to sustain a frank conversation, we tend to arrive at higher-quality decisions, including many that surprise people. We entered one of our strategy retreats talking casually about moving our business onto the cloud. We left it resolved to make an aggressive push. During our 2015 retreat, someone proposed the idea of polling customers in the early stages of our software implementations. Until then, we had waited until the end of implementations to query them on satisfaction—and at that point, there was no longer much we could do to have an impact. This change led to significant, measurable improvements in customer satisfaction. That same year, our business serving small and midsize customers emerged as a central focus of our conversations, whereas previously we had discussed it only marginally.

Perhaps the biggest, most momentous surprise to have come out of our planning retreat was verticalization. As I mentioned in Chapter 3, at our 2009 planning retreat, one of our leaders broached the idea of verticalizing more of our sales force. At the time, we had sales teams dedicated to two specific industries, healthcare and retail. The rest of our salespeople covered an array of industries across geographies. At the outset of our retreat, nobody could have foreseen that we would have resolved to verticalize the rest of the company—it was hardly a consensus view. The move seemed poised to disrupt the company, as it required our sales teams to reconfigure how they operated. A number of people on my leadership team registered skepticism, and even outright opposition to the idea. Finance was not a big fan, worrying that verticalization would lead to inefficiencies and higher costs. For instance, we might now face situations in which three different people traveled to a particular city at a time, serving customers in different industries, whereas previously only one salesperson would have had to make the trip. On the other hand, marketing argued that verticalization would render our communications sharper and more effective, since we would be speaking to more targeted audiences.

As we debated the question, more of us moved toward the pro-verticalization camp. The numbers didn't lie: all of our sales teams had experienced declines in sales during the 2008 recession, except for the verticalized teams. Why was that? Well, verticalized teams become experts in their industries, providing more value to customers. Some of our toughest competitors were smaller companies whose products served just one industry. As a matter of fact, we had created a verticalized healthcare team during the 1990s precisely because our sales team was having difficulty with a smaller, more specialized player.

By the end of the retreat, enough people—including me— found pro-verticalization arguments so compelling that we decided to pursue the strategy, despite the risk of disruption and other uncertainties. It was a bold move that we never would have made had we not brought people from different disciplines together to hash it out. If we had left it to our sales executives to make the call, they would have chosen not to verticalize. But sometimes you need a bit of distance to do what's right for the entire organization. To his credit, our head of sales listened carefully to all of the pro-verticalization arguments, and even though some of his team leaders may have been uncomfortable, he wound up leading the charge within his group.

Verticalization might have been the single most important strategic decision Kronos has yet enacted. It single-handedly turbocharged our growth and is a primary reason our revenues topped $1 billion. Afterward, when we won big contracts from large customers and asked them why they chose us, they revealed that it was because we understood the complexities and inner workings of their specific industries.

RESOURCE THE STRATEGY

Once you have a smart, clear strategy in hand, you might think you're all set. You're all revved up, eager to execute—what else is there to do? Well, you have to actually follow up on the strategy.

When you fail to take concerted action on a strategy enough times, people become cynical, seeing strategy as mere jargon and judging that nothing significant will ever change. How many times have you had a meeting with colleagues and planned a project, only to go away and see those plans fail to materialize? That can happen easily with corporate or department-level strategy as well. People get busy. They go back to their daily work and forget all about the larger vision.

The solution is to follow up and mobilize resources behind the strategy so that your people can actually execute it. That's what we do at Kronos. As CEO, I take on the responsibility of holding our organization accountable for the strategy. A couple months after our planning retreats, I'll review the budgets our leaders have drafted for the following year, comparing them to our strategies. Are we allocating enough people or money? If mismatches occur, I don't hesitate to call people out on it. Nor does the finalizing of budgets end our efforts to follow up on the strategy. At the beginning of each year's strategy session, we grade ourselves on how well we executed the previous year's strategic priorities. We candidly discuss our executional weaknesses, and congratulate ourselves on our successes. If we're not executing parts of our strategy well, we want to know why. It's the only way we can do better going forward.

EVANGELIZE THE STRATEGY

You can be the greatest strategic thinker on the planet, and your team can devise ideal budgets, but if you don't know how to communicate your strategy to broader groups of employees—and not just communicate it but galvanize people around it—you won't execute on the strategy well and foster engagement. At Kronos, we focus on communicating the strategy from its very inception. On the final day of our retreat, we typically spend time figuring out how best to summarize our decisions and communicate them to the rest of the company. We feel it's important to align ourselves behind the same message. Sometimes it will take us hours to agree on the exact verbiage.

From there, we mount a months-long internal campaign to communicate the strategy to every corner of the organization. I assume a lead role, talking about the strategy wherever I go as if it were my full-time job (which it is!). I present the strategy formally to large groups of Kronites at annual departmental kickoff meetings, as well as at smaller team meetings. Depending on the Kronites with whom I'm speaking, I describe the specific ways that a particular team supports our strategy. And always, I convey my own genuine excitement about the strategy. Other members of our leadership team also communicate the strategy in their departments and business units.

In some cases, other leaders and I draft internal communications that distill the essence of a strategy to Kronites, explain our thinking, and request participation. In 2017, for instance, we saw an opportunity to make our business more efficient by reducing wasteful spending. We paid more than $40 million annually to buy licenses and subscriptions for software tools that Kronites used, but we found that many employees weren't actually using these tools. A review we performed of our travel spending found that many Kronites were taking unnecessary trips, not always buying airplane tickets in accordance with our policy, and failing to book hotel rooms using preferred rates we had negotiated. Since we lacked a global policy governing when Kronites could hold meetings and other events that required travel, many in-person meetings were being organized that might have been handled remotely, and they were being held in more expensive locales when cheaper options were available. We also looked at a number of other areas where we might reduce costs, such as our practices relating to payment terms with our customers and the use of consultants and contractors.

To communicate our new strategy of cost containment, I wrote to Kronites explaining that "our spending growth in recent years has outpaced our revenue growth," a disparity that had become unsustainable. I asked Kronites to be "vigilant" in every kind of spending. "Just as every Kronite plays a role in helping us deliver a superior experience to our customers, building great products, and sustaining our admirable revenue growth track record, we are now asking every Kronite to play a part by helping us optimize our recent investments." Our chief financial officer, Mark, followed up with communications dedicated to discussing several areas of excessive spending, as well as measures we were introducing to tighten our purse strings, including stricter policies, entirely new policies, and more oversight (such as creation of a software asset management program). As leaders, we had an ability to spotlight this strategy for our employees so that they could remain mindful of it and help us reach our goals. The stakes were huge: if we could get Kronites to spend more thoughtfully, not just by forcing it through oversight measures but by inspiring it through communications, we could cut millions of dollars of waste from our budget. Our efforts seem to be paying off. We cut our travel expenses by over $1 million, our spending on software licenses by over $1 million, and our spending on contractors and consultants by over 10 percent without impacting our effectiveness.

Members of our leadership team are hardly the only ones communicating our strategy. Many others inside Kronos do as well, helping to cascade the strategy down through the ranks. After we present the strategy at departmental kickoff meetings at the start of our fiscal year, senior leaders meet with their direct reports to review the strategy and set goals against it. Those direct reports meet with their teams, all the way down through the organization. Cascading enables managers to lead their team with a strong sense of direction, one that has been carefully considered and that is based on hard data. It's extremely important for every Kronite to understand how his or her role contributes to our "greater good," to our strategic vision. This is where the real "magic" of strategy is applied to engagement. If you can get each individual Kronite to understand how his or her activities support the company and its goals, they'll all be more inspired from the moment they first arrive at work in the morning.

At this point, our branding and strategy "wrappers" help infuse the entire workplace with our strategy. Kronites around the world post our strategy collateral in their workspaces so that they can see it every day as they work. We also present our strategy in its branded form to all new hires, suggesting that they ask their managers how their own, specific role connects with it. I can't emphasize enough how helpful the branding of our strategy has been inside Kronos. For years before we introduced it, employees did the best they could to support our corporate plans, but those plans might not have been front and center in their minds, and employees didn't necessarily perceive their own personal connection to Kronos's goals and success. Now they do, and it gives them a far greater sense of meaning.

In addition to communicating the strategy itself, we expose every employee to the *impact* our organization has on customers as a result of our strategies. We call this our Customer-First focus. We convene customer advisory boards and solicit candid customer feedback about our products. We also hold "InterAct" sessions in which we invite customers to speak with large groups of Kronites to describe how our software helps their organization.

At one presentation, a representative from a large public school system related how Kronos solutions improved teacher attendance and alleviated administrative burdens, leading to better school performance and enhanced learning outcomes for children in the district. This story really resonated with Kronites, reminding them that the work they do benefits people all over the world in a variety of ways.

MAKE STRATEGY HAPPEN

To create an environment in which people love what they do, you don't need to embrace a strategy planning process that replicates the one I've outlined here. Simply focus on talking about strategy with others in your organization in a productive and inspiring way. If you manage a team, do you connect with your team periodically, thinking together about how you might work differently and where you should invest your resources? Do you take care to include a variety of viewpoints, not just people who might agree with your vision? Do you have vigorous debate before coalescing around a manageable number of priorities? Do you follow up afterward, making sure your budgeting reflects your strategies? Do you communicate the strategy, making it a tangible part of every employee's workday and spurring two-way dialogue about strategy and its execution? If not, then you might find these ideas helpful.

Strategy ultimately isn't profound or mysterious. You just have to do it—and yes, you have to be involved in the details of its communication. By making the effort to frame a strategy in a rigorous way and then evangelizing it, you'll open the way for all of your employees to experience more meaning and purpose at work, and thus to become more engaged. Don't forget to give your employees a voice in strategy formation, too. Although leaders and managers primarily frame strategy at Kronos, we include other individuals within the company each year, and our data collection processes described earlier take into account information about employee perceptions. Once our strategy is framed, employees also contact me with concerns and comments about it, and I ask as many of them as I can what they think of it. You see, I *like* talking about our strategy with employees. I'm excited about what we're doing as a company, and I want them to be, too. I also like hearing their feedback. Our company owes its employees a good, honest strategy, one that they find credible, so that they can come together around a single, animating purpose and do their best work.

Why do I worry so much about the nuances of our strategic "wrappers" and everything else that touches our strategy? Because I care about the happiness, enthusiasm, and dedication of our workforce. Many good things arise out of hope, but engagement requires a clear, cogent vision of the path ahead, and a plan to get there. So, enough talk. If you, your team, and your organization haven't spent enough time lately thinking about strategy, then get started!

6

Have Fun

In 2014, we launched one of the most memorable products in our history. It was called Workforce Home, and it promised to revolutionize the way people around the world ran their households. As we realized, many parents felt bogged down by the complexity of scheduling their kids' after-school activities. They were tired of pestering their kids to do their homework or perform chores, and they needed help transporting the right family member to the right place at the right time. Workforce Home allowed users to solve these and many similar problems quickly, with just a few swipes on their mobile devices.

To help promote Workforce Home, we issued a press release, as we do with all of our product launches. Using language familiar to Kronites everywhere, the release touted the software's "hundreds of productivity-improving features," including "advanced scheduling," "task management," and "workflows."[1] In essence, we took the rich functionality and ease of use of our workforce management solutions and applied them to the home. I was so excited about Workforce Home that on April 1, I sent an e-mail to our entire company gushing about it. I congratulated all Kronites who had helped make the product a reality, noting that it was "truly remarkable how our company [continued] to innovate." I invited Kronites to watch and share a promotional video we'd prepared that introduced the product and dramatized its use (check out the video at https://youtu.be/x5LepNJc9EQ).

The response from Kronites and customers was amazing. The video has been viewed over 10,000 times on our website and social media channels. One Kronite wrote to our communications team, "At first, I wasn't sure if this was real, but then after viewing the link I can see that it is. Is there any way I can help pilot this product? Looks very interesting and incredibly innovative." Others were somewhat annoyed. A few of our service people e-mailed me to ask why we hadn't trained them on the product before releasing it. "How the heck am I going to support this product?" one of them asked. Still other Kronites—the majority—were incredulous. Software for the workplace was one thing, but did people really need to "optimize" the "productivity" of their homes? Had Kronos really devoted resources to developing workforce management software for the home?

No, we hadn't. It was all an elaborate April Fools' joke—one that employees to this day still talk about.

To create a culture and a workplace that people love, it's important to humanize the organization and infuse it with levity and *personality*. So many companies seem gripped by excessive formality. Daily experience is tedious and bland, sometimes to the point of feeling dehumanizing. Why does work have to be so serious? Yes, we want employees to work hard and perform, and daily operations at Kronos and in most other organizations will involve a certain amount of drudgery and tedium. But why can't a company foster a unique and lighthearted spirit as well? Why can't we make it *fun* to come to work?

That was the thinking behind our April Fools' prank, and it informs a number of events and other culture-building efforts we support each year. We try to keep it fun, and also to "keep it real"—to evoke a sense of authenticity at work. Sometimes concocting a good-natured prank is precisely what is required to infuse personality and fun on an organizational level. But if you truly want to build engagement, don't stop at the organizational level. Be yourself each day at work. Have fun. Let your hair down a little, even if it means sometimes breaking the rules. And always tell the truth. Your people will appreciate the authenticity of your words and actions. They'll believe in you because they'll feel they know you—the real you. Your personal brand and the company's brand will become humanized. Employee engagement and affection for the company will increase in turn.

THE MANY FACES OF FUN

In loosening up your culture, it's important to give employees a chance to express their own personalities and enjoy themselves. An obvious place to start is with your workplace and lifestyle amenities. Silicon Valley is famous for its perks and amenities, including free meals, slippers to wear around the office, special spaces for music performances, and so on. When designing our new headquarters, we thought long and hard about how we could best build enjoyment into the workday and dedicated an entire floor to fun and collaboration—what we call "we" space. There's a gaming area, a parklike space complete with swings, a high-end coffee and smoothie bar, a library, a variety of food options, board games, walking workstations, and fitness classes.

As Kronites are discovering, it's a lot easier to lighten up and let your personality out when you're sipping a mocha latte with your teammates or enjoying a game of air hockey. As one employee wrote: "The workspaces, the conference rooms, the colors, the lighting . . . everything is awesome!"

Wellness programs provide another opportunity for the building of authentic work relationships. We offer an array of initiatives under our global LiveInspired wellness program, not just the usual options focused on diet, exercise, and smoking cessation, but seminars on the healing power of laughter, a "March Madness" exercise challenge (which I did *not* win), a "Virtual Torch Walk Around the Globe" walking competition, an obstacle course challenge, company-sponsored running races, a chance to play on our cricket team (at our locations in India), and numerous seasonal events. As one Kronite posted on our internal collaboration site, "I'm lucky enough to work in an environment where we smile every day, we laugh, we have jokes, and we make fun times as good as we can and work alongside the hard times."

Many of our functional departments also have committees devoted specifically to fun. Stop into our offices throughout the year, and you'll see Kronites participating in Halloween decorating competitions, pie-eating contests, special days when employees dress up in themed costumes, cookoff competitions, and many more. On our internal collaboration platform, we've run a number of lighthearted contests, including a "best selfie" photo competition for interns, a pet photo contest, and a "Cubespiration" competition in which Kronites tell us their personal tricks for staying inspired on the job. We also hold an annual Take Your Child to Work Day, including lighthearted events and special programs for the children of Kronites. A longstanding tradition is free breakfast Fridays, at which Kronites spend time together laughing and talking about the week's events and the weekend ahead.

Collectively, the stream of events, initiatives, and programs convey that Kronos is a different kind of company—a place where each employee can be him- or herself, and where work isn't always so serious. Kronos itself takes on a "personality," one of friendliness, authenticity, and relaxed sociability. In the wake of our April Fools' joke, for instance, many employees and customers wrote to let us know how delighted they were with the company's levity. "Kronos just got WAY cooler," one customer said. As a Kronite remarked, "I love working for a company that has a sense of humor." Another Kronite playfully asked, "Is *this* what's going to get us over a billion dollars?"

Our corporate communications further the notion of Kronos as a different kind of workplace, with our official Kronos cartoon, started in 2010. Called "Time Well Spent" and created by noted cartoonist Tom Fishburne, the cartoon comes out weekly, playing up humorous aspects of what it takes to manage a workforce in any organization. Managing a workforce is pretty complex, with many issues to consider, like compliance, scheduling, human resources, payroll, compensation, and so on. Yet it doesn't always have to *feel* like such a massive undertaking.

By all accounts, our employees appreciate our "Time Well Spent" cartoons (see figure on page 102). To date, the cartoons have been viewed 3.6 million times and have spurred hundreds of likes, comments, and shares on social media. Employees use the cartoons in their presentations, and we also put them on notepads, calendars, totes, and the like for giveaways at our customer meetings. We've run cartoon caption contests and erected green screens before which Kronites and customers could pose so that they could star in the cartoons themselves. And employees and customers aren't the only ones who like the cartoons: other employers sometimes request permission to borrow them for use in their own organizations.

An example of a "Time Well Spent" cartoon

BE YOURSELF

As important as organizational or departmental initiatives are, you as a leader and manager set the tone. If you want a sense of authentic personality to reign in the workplace, project one yourself. In Chapter 2, I discussed the importance of honesty and transparency in communications. You certainly can't achieve authenticity without them. But the style of your communication and behavior matters, too. Leaders and managers sometimes feel that they have to leave their "true" selves at home. They occupy positions of authority, so in their minds they have to convey that authority every minute they're on the job—otherwise, they surrender it. These leaders and managers might be polite or cordial around colleagues, exchanging pleasantries, but they remain guarded, keenly aware of all those unspoken boundaries that permeate workplaces and govern social interactions.

I have nothing against more formal leadership or management styles. Nobody has *the* recipe for success, certainly not me. What I've found, though, is that unleashing your personality in the workplace, perhaps even in unexpected ways, can go a long way toward giving an organization a personality and keeping engagement high. It's also much easier, simpler, and less stressful to "be yourself" at work, rather than constantly worrying about playing a part—and doing so perfectly—in others' presence.

Let me give you an example of what I mean. There I was, at a fiscal year kickoff meeting presenting to sales and service employees about our company strategy, our culture, and a suite of new benefits we were launching. One of the slides in my deck referenced our pet insurance offering. "Did you know we offer pet insurance?" I blurted out to Kronites. "I didn't know that. My family could really use it! We have a crazy dog, a Jack Russell Terrier named Sammy." I went on for a few more minutes to talk about my dog and how my wife and I, after an appointment with a specialist, put Sammy on an antidepressant to calm him down. After I presented, I posted a photo of Sammy in the conference app so everyone could see what he looked like. This prompted many Kronites to post photos of their cherished pets, too.

Every day when I come to work, I try to bring my whole self. When a group of younger Kronites is riding on the elevator and I get on, I sometimes break the ice by saying something like, "Oh, great, I'm so glad to be on this elevator, which is stopping on every floor. I'm going to have you all trapped here. You're going to have to talk to me for the whole ride up!" Once when I addressed a group of our engineers, including some who had worked on a plum project (a big new product we were launching), I said, "I really apologize to all you guys on the new product team. It doesn't produce any money and does nothing to contribute to our bonuses this year. I know you guys feel terrible about that." This isn't high comedy by any means, but it's spontaneous, it reflects my unvarnished feelings and personality, and it elicits a chuckle or two from employees.

In public settings, I'll often spontaneously poke fun at Kronites or others, just to lighten the mood and because I genuinely like them. At one event, I was standing on a stage in front of about 3,000 people introducing one of our customers. When he stood up, I was surprised by his height. "Wow, you're so tall," I blurted out. Not necessarily what the audience expected, but they were seeing the "real" me. I then went on to utter a few self-deprecating remarks about the benefits of being a vertically challenged man.

During a press interview with the *Boston Globe* in 2010, I spontaneously used the term "Yikes-a-roo." I'm not even sure where that came from! Wouldn't you know it, the journalist referenced the phrase in the article's first sentence, writing, "It's not just any chief executive who uses the phrase 'yikes-a-roo.' But somehow Aron Ain manages to pull it off." How do I pull it off? Not because I have some special talent or gift. Because I don't care! I didn't worry very much about what the journalist or readers of that article might think of me. I was more concerned with just being myself with the journalist, as I am with everyone. I can't go through life parsing out every word and self-censoring. That sounds miserable to me. So I don't even try.

I've cited some funny examples, but authenticity in communications isn't always funny. Sometimes it's pure communication in the moment, clear and to the point. When I'm serving on a panel, people will occasionally ask me a question, assuming that I know the answer, when in truth I don't. "Aron," they'll say, "you have experience with this." Rather than pose or posture, I'll simply tell it like it is: "Actually, I don't." Likewise, when I'm giving feedback to Kronites, I tell them what they need to hear, even if it risks startling them. Let's say I'm unhappy with how a member of my team behaved during a meeting. I'll pull him or her aside right after the meeting and be very direct. "What was that all about?" I'll ask. "You were being a jerk. You were acting like you knew everything, and like nobody else had a valid opinion. Could you please go apologize to the people you were being a jerk to?" Usually, the team member will own his or her behavior, make amends, and we'll all move on. Clear feedback delivered without a lot of scripting or massaging in the moment can make all the difference.

I don't want to suggest that the majority of what I do or say is spontaneous or unpolished. I read the room like any leader or manager, and I'll sometimes make adjustments when necessary. I'll also sometimes repeat messages that I've delivered before. When I have the opportunity to speak with a group of Kronites, I often tell them, "Go home and hug your family members and your pets, tell them that you love them, and thank them for allowing you to put so much energy and enthusiasm into your work." Likewise, I consistently ask people I meet about their families—again and again and again. Kronites have come to expect it, but since I really do care about people's families—since concern about family goes to the core of my values and who I am—the question is an authentic one.

Despite such repetition, my public presentations, media interviews, and recorded videos tend to strike people as freewheeling, primarily because I don't use notes or a teleprompter. "Aron Unplugged," one of my colleagues calls it. Many people ask me how I do it. My little secret: I prepare like crazy! I believe that one way to convey authenticity as an executive or manager might well be precisely (and paradoxically) to *over*prepare.

Like many other leaders, I work with a team of communications professionals who help me craft and fact-check my message, and in the case of media interviews, brief me thoroughly on the interviewer beforehand. If I have a big speech, I'll sit for hours beforehand, sometimes days, reviewing any material, thinking through what I want to say, and plotting out a rough outline in my head. I'll run through the presentation repeatedly to make sure I understand it. Each time I do, the ideas come out slightly differently. Still, by the time I step on stage, I feel firmly in command of my material—so much so that I can talk without notes and make adjustments to my speech on the spot, as the ideas occur to me and in response to the energy in the room.

Intense preparation *facilitates* spontaneity. It's a lot easier to relax in public and say what comes to mind if you're steeped in a subject and understand in advance the primary points or messages you wish to convey.

THE DOWNSIDE OF AUTHENTICITY

Does authentic communication carry any downsides for leaders and managers? Not really. It's all upside. Did I mention that authenticity facilitates trust (Chapter 3)? Another big upside: authenticity is the *right* thing to do. Do you like it when someone is trying to "handle" you, put on an act, tell you exactly what you want to hear? I know I don't. So how could I in good conscience impose that on others around me, even just a little bit?

You might fear that in letting your guard down just a little bit (and that's all I'm advocating, a little bit) you'll say or do the wrong thing, creating headaches for yourself or others. That's valid. During one interview with the *Boston Business Journal*, I inadvertently revealed that we were looking at possibly relocating our headquarters. The reporter observed how rapidly our company was growing, and I said something to the effect of "Yes, actually we're looking at maybe relocating. We're going to stay in the Merrimack Valley [of Massachusetts]." Our communications team was concerned: if employees who worked at our head-quarters found out about this move from a media article, they might have become anxious that their commutes would become longer. They also might have felt disconnected from our leader-ship to be hearing the news secondhand. Our communications team leapt into action, drafting an e-mail from me to all of our Massachusetts-based employees making the announcement and explaining our decision. We sent the e-mail moments after the *Boson Business Journal* article appeared—problem averted!

As our head of communications tells me, "It's always an adventure staffing your media interviews!" An adventure, yes, but a big problem? No. I accept that I might not always say the right things in the moment, and that my communications team or I might have to circle back later to pick up the pieces. I also accept that while many Kronites love how open and honest I am, others probably wish I would tone it down with the media, customers, or others outside the company. I am who I am! I'm going to do what I'm going to do, hopefully with enough emo-tional intelligence not to say anything *too* dumb. I've never made any big boo-boos while expressing my personality. When you consider the great benefits that come with it, including better relationships with employees and enhanced employee engage-ment, it's clear—to me, at least—that the risk of an occasional inconvenience is well worth taking.

EASING INTO AUTHENTICITY

An outgoing, expressive approach to communications happens to be my style, but it isn't for every manager, and it certainly isn't an absolute requirement for employees to enjoy work. One of our highest-rated managers at Kronos is by temperament quiet and formal. He doesn't easily say what's on his mind, and in general listens more than he talks. Yet he's a great leader and an authentic one. Different approaches—even those that are diametrically opposed—can yield similar results. You as a manager or leader need to find your own path. My argument is simply that if you care about engaging employees, it's well worth taking a posture of relative openness in your on-the-job behavior, whatever that might mean to you.

You might counter that you already do have close, transparent, authentic relationships in place with others around you. Perhaps you do. But don't take it for granted. Do you *really* know how your team members feel about their relationship with you and the company? When you're making formal presentations, how free-flowing are you *really*? Are you thinking too much about what you're saying, and are you censoring yourself? When you're interacting one-on-one with teammates, are you as lighthearted as you might be? Are you having fun? Or is there a yawning gap between your demeanor at home and at work? Is your work more stressful than it has to be—because you're making it that way? Are you taking yourself too seriously? Spend some time thinking about these questions. Return repeatedly to them over a few weeks, letting them sink in. And if you do conclude that you have work to do in this area, then don't hesitate—get started!

If you've never let your personality truly shine at work because you've worried about stepping on toes or embarrassing yourself, put those concerns aside and just *try* it. Try it once, maybe with a few people you like or with whom you feel comfortable. If you like the results and how *you* feel in the moment, gradually increase the number of settings or occasions in which you let down your guard. Mind you, don't let your guard all the way down. Let it down a little bit, and then a little bit more, delicately feeling out how far you can reasonably go. If you occasionally stray over the line, don't stress too much about it. Pick up the pieces and move on, reminding yourself of authenticity's great benefits.

A gradual approach is probably best when trying to infuse personality into your larger organization or team. In the drive to make your workplace more relaxed and fun, don't feel you have to do everything all at once. Start with a couple of initiatives, and go from there. Solicit your team's ideas, and involve them in planning and execution. Create a dedicated "fun" committee. None of this has to cost a lot of money. Our Halloween competition, in which teams vie to create the most elaborately decorated space, is great fun and a wonderful team-building experience, and costs very little. In 2017, we gave each floor at our headquarters a $250 allowance, and the grand prize for the winning floor was a pizza party. Our people were thrilled to participate, and they brought their enthusiasm back to their jobs, making our small investment more than worth it.

I really do believe that having fun can help you forge better relationships with your employees, leading to higher engagement and a better business overall. And hey, if you don't believe me, well, I've got a subscription to Workplace Home I'd like to sell you. Trust me, it's the best productivity optimization tool you'll ever buy for your home. You and your family will never be the same!

7

Astonish Them
with Kindness

In 2017, a Kronite named Adam used our internal collaboration platform to contact fellow Kronites with an important request. A month earlier, his 15-year-old-nephew Sullivan had been diagnosed with leukemia. To cheer up his nephew, Sullivan's mother thought that it might be nice if he received postcards from all 50 U.S. states. Adam wrote asking his fellow Kronites for help. Would his colleagues, located throughout the country and the world, be willing to send a postcard to Sullivan?

The answer was a resounding yes. Within minutes, Kronites in states such as California, Illinois, New Hampshire, North Carolina, Texas, and Wisconsin wrote back promising to send postcards, as did employees in countries such as Canada, Germany, and the United Kingdom. Of the 9,000 postcards Sullivan received, many were from Kronites. The outpouring was so great that it prompted our chief people officer to chime in with a comment on our culture of caring. "I'm not at all surprised to hear that Kronites from around the globe rallied to your cause," he said to Adam. "Kronos is a special place exactly because of the huge hearts of the fantastic people who work here. It's been my experience that Kronites take care of each other in good times and in trying times. Especially when it comes to taking care of family members in need."

I deeply appreciate Kronites' eagerness to take care of one another. Kronites often cite a sense of feeling cared for—of feeling part of a family—when describing why they love to work here. And as they observe, warmth and compassion are evident in the course of daily work, not just at times of crisis. "I never [before] worked for a company . . . where people will bend over backward to help you succeed," one Kronite said. As another told us, "I feel like I'm a member of a giant family. Kronites appreciate each other not only for what we can achieve but for who we are as people. Kronites encourage one another to be the best they can be. We help each other learn and grow. That is what makes Kronos truly unique." A third Kronite who left the company, worked elsewhere, and then returned to Kronos (a not uncommon phenomenon we discuss in Chapter 10) related that the experience had left him even more aware of Kronos's unique culture. "I didn't realize how much I missed my Kronos family. Yes, family."

Every organization has its share of good, caring people who help their colleagues. But you don't often find a strong, cohesive *culture* of caring. What's noteworthy about Adam's request and the response it elicited is precisely how *unremarkable* they are at Kronos. In the 2017 Great Place to Work Trust Index Survey, 92 percent of Kronites polled agreed with the statement that "people care about each other here."[1] And for good reason: our employees around the world respond with kindness all the time, usually without being asked. When one of our employees was deployed to Kuwait, his colleagues regularly sent care packages to remind him that he was in his team's thoughts and prayers. Another Kronite had a son with congenital heart problems requiring frequent trips to the emergency room. Whenever these last-minute emergencies arose, the team pulled together to cover their fellow Kronite so this parent could focus on what mattered most: family. Quite often, a Kronite will learn of a colleague's personal setbacks and inform other employees, who spontaneously contribute money, write letters of support, or offer some other form of assistance. Even employees who don't know the affected Kronite routinely step up.

Although our company has always sought to treat employees well, we've worked hard in recent years to embed strong values of caring and compassion into our organization. Through formal policies and communications, we've articulated our expectation that Kronites not only perform well on the job, but also treat one another with kindness and respect. We've consciously set a strong example of caring for employees to follow, implementing a range of policies that care for "the whole person." As I'll describe in this chapter, we've mobilized company resources to care for employees in times of crisis, to an extent that astonishes Kronites and sets the company apart in their eyes as a uniquely wonderful place to work.

Caring and compassion might sound much too "soft" to represent a business tactic. Isn't that just a bunch of human resources talk? I would counter that cultivating a spirit of kindness at work is fundamental to maximizing your business success. As we've seen, when a culture of caring takes root, and when it's placed on near-equal footing with raw performance, loyalty, commitment, and engagement skyrocket. But I don't need data to prove the business value of caring—it's common sense. Would you rather work in a culture where people tear one another down, or where they show kindness and lift one another up? Would you be more inclined to treat customers well if your colleagues ignored or disrespected you, or if they actively valued you? And from an organizational standpoint, is it easier and more productive to show people kindness, or to treat them indifferently or callously? Would you rather lead a team of people who collaborate and challenge one another because they've built up trust through acts of caring and kindness, or a team of people who are afraid to speak their minds because of gossip and backstabbing?

Creating a workplace where people feel inspired to achieve excellence is simpler than people think. You don't need to dangle rewards or rely on a punitive "up or out" system. Mobilize altruism as a lever, inspiring your people to treat others with dignity and respect. Creating a company that's not just another workplace but a true family or team might be one of the best long-term moves you can make to improve your bottom line. Altruism certainly helped us to reach a billion dollars. Today, it's taking us even further.

NOT JUST A COMPANY—A *HOME*

One of the most important steps you can take to cultivate norms of caring is to articulate firm expectations about behavior at every turn. At new employee orientations, we communicate our caring ethos through a visual communications tool called Kronos Home. In 2015, we decided that we needed a simple but inspiring way to articulate what it means to be a Kronite. After reviewing employee engagement surveys, focus groups, and general feedback about why Kronites love the company, we developed Kronos Home. The foundation for the home was the concepts of trust and transparency. The rest of the home visual consists of four quadrants, "care for our families," "care for our communities," "care for our customers," and "care for each other."

We present "care for each other" to new employees as a signature value of the Kronos workspace—every bit as important as the other three elements (discussed in other chapters). As we explain, our emphasis on caring is reflected in numerous employee benefits the company offers, including wellness programming, a student loan repayment assistance offering, an open time off policy, pet insurance benefit, and many others. But mostly, we focus on creating a corporate environment where we simultaneously care for one another and produce great results.

We know it's not enough for new Kronites to hear about caring in the abstract—they also need to *experience* it. Even before Kronites' first days on the job, their managers and team members often welcome them with small acts of kindness. One new Kronite remarked during the interview process that he had a new baby. Our team sent a bouquet of flowers with a note of congratulations to his family. Another described a sick loved one. Once again, we sent a small gift. In another instance, a hiring manager invited a new Kronite to have lunch with her a week before her start date. Starting a new job can be stressful as well as exciting, so Kronites try to make the experience as positive as possible, making a statement in the process about our culture and values. They reinforce the message on Kronites' first days of work, introducing themselves, decorating the new Kronite's workspace, writing individual notes of welcome, inviting new Kronites to yoga classes or lunchtime basketball games, and offering other personal gestures of friendship and camaraderie.

Such gestures are small, but as new Kronites have told us, they make a big difference. "The culture is amazing," one new

Kronite said. "I like working for a company that truly values its employees and shows it." Another expressed happiness at having "a manager and team who really cares, not just about your work life but your personal life." In the eyes of new Kronites, expressions of caring sharply distinguish the company from others they've worked for. In the words of a new Kronite: "It is refreshing to work for a company that not only puts its customers first but does so because employees are valued in such a way that they are actually happy."

To encourage employees to treat others compassionately, you must create incentives that reinforce the behavior as a regular operating norm. Our bonus program, for which all Kronites are eligible, rewards Kronites for behaving well toward their colleagues in the course of their daily work. Put differently, it rewards *how* work gets done, not just the achievement of performance goals. Specifically, in calculating a Kronite's job performance, we allocate 40 percent of the score to reflect how well a Kronite displayed our core values of character, competence, and collaboration. Did the Kronite motivate others to excel? Did he or she treat others fairly and respectfully? Did he or she work to gain others' trust? Did he or she give others credit for their accomplishments? Our core values don't explicitly say "treat Kronites like family," but that's implicit. Kronite salary increases are directly tied to how they embody our culture of caring while "working inspired" to drive results.

And when Kronites don't behave in ways that reflect our values, we are forced to levy negative consequences. In the interests of "winning," many companies will tolerate employees who behave like jerks so long as they're high performers. Not us. In recruiting new hires, we try to hire people who seem to treat others respectfully, as we believe that culture fit is just as important as role fit, *if not more important.* We coach hiring managers how to evaluate prospective employees' communication style, inter-personal skills, values, and work habits, determining whether they are commensurate with our culture. On a job-seeker web-site, one Kronos candidate recently wrote, "I was very surprised by how many of the questions were directed toward culture and fit. It is important to Kronos to put the right people in the right seats, and not just fill the seats."

Sometimes we err, hiring people whose behavior doesn't fit with our culture. In these instances, we let the people go—and don't think twice about it, even if they are high performers. Any short-term gain we might accrue by virtue of having high-performing employees like these is more than offset by the damage these individuals would inflict on our company culture. By acting decisively, we send a message: treating other Kronites well is paramount.

Kronites notice when we penalize bad behavior and when we maintain benefits and other policies that care for employees. But what might make the strongest impression of all is how we step up in times of crisis. I've described how individual Kronites help their colleagues endure challenging times. The organiza-tion does the same. Many companies have formal policies that pay out certain benefits when accident, death, or illness strike a family. These benefits are typically based on the employee's tenure with the company. We take a more informal approach. Because we don't create formulas for people and the situations they're going through, they feel like individuals. Every case is dif-ferent, and our policy is to treat them that way.

When something bad happens to a Kronite, fellow employees are moved to action. They alert their managers, and in this way the news quickly makes it to our human resources team, which determines what an individual Kronite needs to face the crisis at hand. We then decide what help to offer, without a lengthy decision-making process. If an employee is in trouble and we can help, we do, and swiftly.

One day in the summer of 2017, a Kronite named Lisa lost her house to a catastrophic fire. Her family was OK, but they had nowhere to go. That afternoon, one of Lisa's colleagues paid her a visit, saying that she had a donation from the company to give her. This colleague gave Lisa a check for $5,000, enough to pay for a hotel, clothing, food, and other short-term needs. We also sent her a computer to use, since hers had been destroyed in the fire. "When I saw what they had for me, I was completely blown away," Lisa said. "They had that money in my hands before the insurance company did."

Unfortunately, the fire wasn't the end of Lisa's travails that year. About a month later, her father passed away after a prolonged illness. In the obituary, Lisa's family announced that well-wishers could make donations to the Massachusetts Society for the Prevention of Cruelty to Animals (MSPCA), since her father had always loved animals. Soon after, Lisa received a card from the MSPCA informing her that Kronos had made a donation in her father's name. She was blown away all over again. "[The help I received] was just constant," she said. She further noted that "during a year of crisis, I never met with any kind of disdain or jealousy that I was getting special treatment. My coworkers all stepped up to do whatever they could. It was just complete support all the way up the chain."

In another instance, a Kronite whom I'll call Michael was diagnosed with a terminal illness. At many companies, managers and colleagues might express sympathy and arrange for more time off. We did that—and more. On his own initiative, Michael's manager reached out to colleagues to collect funds so that Michael's family could travel to Disney World together. Employees, including many who didn't know Michael, rushed to donate. Days after we learned of Michael's diagnosis, we surprised him and his family with a check for more than $9,000. Again, this specific response isn't mandated by a formal policy in our employee handbook. But it exemplifies our individualized approach to employee care.

A skeptic might hear me talk about a caring culture and say, "Yes, but hasn't Kronos laid people off in the past? How do you reconcile that with the culture?" It's not easy. Let me be clear: we absolutely *hate* to let Kronites go, and we do everything possible to avoid doing so. Still, we recognize that downsizing in some areas of our business in line with shifting demand is sometimes necessary to keep the larger organization healthy. When we do have to let people go, we do it in accordance with our values, often offering severance packages and other benefits that go beyond what other companies typically give.

To date, I don't believe that layoffs have significantly damaged Kronos's brand with our employees. When many companies downsize, employees often leave embittered, taking the layoff personally. While I'm sure that some ex-Kronites feel this way, I'm struck by the number of ex-Kronites who reapply to work at our company after being laid off. When we let go several dozen employees in 2017 due to changes in specific parts of our business, many of these Kronites reapplied for new positions on our website almost immediately. As a Kronite commented, "When people here are let go, they . . . understand it was a business decision, and yet they still want to be a part of this culture." Letting people go will never be pleasant, but it doesn't have to contaminate a culture. We're not by any means a perfect company, but we do what we can to care for employees, especially in difficult times. It helps, too, that we've laid a foundation of trust and transparency, and that I and other leaders have been overcommunicating all along.

CARING AND COMPASSION
STARTS WITH *YOU*

So far, I've examined steps an organization can take to inject altruism into the culture. But leaders also have a strong role to play. Showing compassion to our employees reflects my personal values and upbringing, and in particular, the example set by my parents. When I was a kid, a woman named Jean who worked for us as a housekeeper fell on hard times. Since she had no place to live, my mother took her in, and Jean wound up living with us for a number of years, sharing a room with my sister, Alice. On another occasion, my uncle, a building inspector, fell off a ladder and broke his leg. We took him in, too, as my roomie! Alice and I never thought that it was odd to share our home with adults who needed help. It was just what our family did to assist and show compassion to a person in need.

But these actions were only the beginning of my parents' efforts in caring for others. My sister remembers how our father took her with him to visit a man struggling with alcoholism in our town. They gave him some support and encouragement, and their presence made his life a little easier. I remember my parents' strong support of an organization called the AHRC that helped individuals with intellectual and other developmental disabilities. Our family didn't have children or relatives with these issues. My parents heard about the organization at a Parent-Teacher Association (PTA) meeting where the founder spoke, and it struck them as a worthy cause in need of support. For decades, my father proudly served on the organization's board, my mother shared her legal knowledge and time as an attorney, and my parents donated seed money to help build a medical clinic to serve that community. Whether it was one person struggling or an organization in need, my parents helped.

Growing up in this environment, I never thought of rendering aid as a choice, much less something particularly worthy of recognition. It was just something you did. If someone needed help, you helped him or her. Today, I apply that thinking to my role as CEO of Kronos. If employees need help, and there's a way that Kronos can offer support, we're going to do that. And if there's a way that I personally can become involved, I'm going to do that, too. I take great satisfaction in lending a hand. But I also know that modeling such generosity through my personal conduct does a great deal to infuse a kind, giving ethos throughout the organization.

What can you as a leader or manager do to put caring on the agenda? For starters, communicate. When I hear that a Kronite has suffered a medical setback or other misfortune, even Kronites whom I don't know personally, I will often send a personal note, sometimes following up with other notes over an extended time period. This doesn't take me long to do, but it's not *pro forma* either—I really give thought to each note. When I later see Kronites in the office, I check in face-to-face to see how they are. I look for other ways to help, too. Because I have served on the board of several hospitals, I'm sometimes in a position to help Kronites secure referrals to expert medical care if necessary. Kronites routinely tell our human resources team how much of a difference this kind of personal involvement makes.

Small gestures often mean the most. When I saw an employee in the hallway whom I knew was going through a difficult divorce, I gave her a hug, asking how she was doing. On another occasion, I spent a half hour in my office with another Kronite talking about a personal situation. "It just makes you cry," one of the Kronites said. "It really does." She understood my behavior as typifying the entire Kronos culture, which was so much more compassionate and focused on her well-being than any of her previous work environments. "When I went to another organization, they cared about me getting the job done. They cared about my skill set and what I could contribute. They didn't care about me as a person. That's what I find here. Kronos cares about *me*."

Like other positive behaviors, caring is contagious. Over the past several years, many other people managers have more firmly embraced caring behaviors. One Kronite, Kim, lost her husband just a few months after returning from maternity leave. Her boss was, in her words, "amazing," offering advice and assistance to help her stabilize her family life. When Kim requested to take a day or two off to be with a visiting family member, her boss insisted she take a week. "It's not just my boss that did that," she said. "I've seen other people go through some tragedies. I just know it's the culture. The loyalty and appreciation I have? You could never get this anywhere [else]."

INSPIRE THEM TO BE THEIR BEST

In 2003, when I was still serving as COO, a Kronite named Dave who also served as a reservist in the military received word that his unit was being deployed to Iraq. Not in a month. Not in a week. The next day. Members of our leadership team were taken aback. We were proud to have a member of the armed forces in our midst, but we also were concerned for Dave's safety.

Dave wasn't an isolated case. During the years after the catastrophic events of September 11, 2001, several other Kronites were also deployed. In each case, we delivered the same message: "Don't worry about your job. It will be waiting for you when you return." Somewhere along the line, I can't remember when exactly, we realized that at a time when hundreds of thousands of U.S. soldiers were deployed overseas, including many reservists who hadn't anticipated being mobilized, just safeguarding these soldiers' jobs wouldn't be enough. During the period of their deployment, they'd receive military pay that was less than their Kronos salaries. How would their families manage? And was it fair that these Kronites would be penalized economically for their service?

We decided that it wasn't, so for several years, we did what to our knowledge few other companies do: on a case-by-case basis—when we were aware of a hardship—we paid the Kronites a supplemental amount to help them during their deployment to minimize this hardship. We didn't publicize this practice. That wasn't why we were doing it. We were doing it because we felt it was the right thing to do, and because it was consistent with our goal of building a strong, caring culture.

Dave served in Iraq for a year, returning in early 2004. He was a combat engineer, doing the dangerous work of disarming improvised explosive devices. When he returned from his deployment, he learned that he'd been promoted and given a raise in his absence. As he recalled, he received an e-mail from us every month while he was away, just checking in, asking how he and his family were doing and whether they needed anything. When he returned, we sent him and his family on a weekend getaway so that he and his family could have a chance to be together and reconnect.

Reflecting back on his deployment, Dave can't emphasize enough what it meant to have Kronos behind him. "We had enough to worry about without worrying about our jobs back home. You've got to keep your mind on what you're doing over there. A lot of soldiers were getting the cold shoulder from their employers. If a soldier is worried about his or her job and supporting their family upon return, he or she is more likely to make a mistake and that is not a good situation for anyone. I never had to deal with that."

It makes me proud as a leader to hear that Dave didn't have to worry about his job. And I know it makes other Kronites just as proud to be part of an organization which, while hardly perfect, is striving constantly to promote every employee's welfare. But these Kronites don't just feel proud. They also contribute more each day on the job. They come to work *inspired*. As Dave said, "When you feel the support in this company, it makes you want to stay up late at night or get up early in the morning just to make sure that customers are getting taken care of."

As I mentioned earlier, we conducted focus groups of Kronites in which we asked them about our culture, including our ethic of caring. During one of these conversations, a Kronite broke down in tears. "Gosh," she said, "this is so embarrassing." Collecting herself, she managed to get a few more words out. "It means a lot to me to work here. I've never worked at a company that's inspired me to be the way that I am as a manager, and just as a person." This woman is the very picture of an engaged, loyal, dedicated employee, simply because her employer goes to considerable lengths to take care of her.

As a leader or manager, what more could you want?

8

Keep Your People Safe

t was November 2016, and Kronites were on edge. Following an incredibly divisive U.S. presidential election, our China and Mexico staff feared that the new administration would deal harshly with them. Some employees who voted conservative felt attacked or marginalized by others who didn't share their beliefs. And Kronites everywhere were concerned about what the future held in store for our company.

I wanted to make sure everyone felt safe, regardless of their beliefs and how they had voted, so I decided to step in. On November 10, two days after the election, I sent an e-mail to Kronites around the world entitled, "Some Thoughts About the U.S. Presidential Election." I acknowledged that the past few months in the United States had been a "very emotional, historic, and politically charged time," and then I got down to my real point, which I wanted every Kronite to understand fully: "Regardless of what transpires in regional or global politics, Kronos will always provide a caring environment that is supportive and encouraging. We will always respect, support, embrace, and take care of each other, our families, our customers, our partners, and our communities." In particular, we would continue to "be fully supportive of our employees of all backgrounds, faiths, and genders, no matter where they live, who they love, or where they worship."

I went on to call upon Kronites to continue to treat one another respectfully, even in moments of disagreement. And I reached out to Kronites in China and Mexico, telling them that they are "an important part of our organization," and that "we will continue to invest in our operations in these regions to grow and support our staff, customers, and partners." Everywhere in the world, we would not let external forces dictate how we behaved. Rather, we would "set our own pace, make our own decisions, and choose the way we do business that creates positivity and unification of spirit and purpose."

Although I worked with my communications team on this e-mail, I didn't spend a great deal of time pondering. It felt like the right thing to do—so I sent it, hoping it would make at least a small difference to Kronites reading it.

Judging from the responses I received, my message made more than a small difference. Hundreds of Kronites from around the world responded expressing gratitude and conveying how touched they were to see the leader of their company send such a reassuring message. One employee reported that my note hit him "in my heart, my brain, my soul." A second said: "This is the absolute BEST 'work' e-mail I have ever received." A number of Kronites who were members of underrepresented or marginalized groups wrote to register the impact my words had. One employee told me that my message, "helps me feel safe and welcomed, and it reassures me that there [are] people [who] care, no matter what."

If you don't take bold stands on external situations affecting your team or organization, I strongly suggest you do so. Some leaders and managers fear saying the wrong thing and offending one group or another. Others believe it is not their place to take stands on issues not directly related to the running of the business. I see it differently. As a leader, I am obliged to help employees feel safe. But setting aside the moral dimension, helping people feel safe is strategically important, one of the most basic tasks leaders and managers must accomplish to build an engaged workforce.

The links between safety, engagement, loyalty to the company, and productivity are no mystery. Employees themselves are aware of it, and in fact, many Kronites took the opportunity to make this connection in their responses to my note about the election. "It is messages such as this that drive our inner passion to do what we do," one Kronite said. Expressing pride in the company, another Kronite pledged to "continue to work hard and help make this company the best it can be for employees and our customers." A third noted that, "This is the kind of culture and understanding that I constantly rave about to my friends and family when speaking about Kronos."

Employees want leaders and managers to stand up for them in times of uncertainty. And it's striking how grateful, loyal, and dedicated they become when you do. If you couple your own communications with organizational policies that set norms of safety and make it an abiding part of the culture, you can bring a whole new level of enthusiasm and inspiration to your workplace.

SPEAKING UP FOR SAFETY

My message responding to the 2016 election wasn't the first time I ventured into political waters to help Kronites feel safe, nor was it by any means the last. In 2015, the state of Indiana passed a law, the Religious Freedom Restoration Act, that many lesbian, gay, bisexual, transgender, and queer (LGBTQ) people felt discriminated against them. In the wake of the law's passage, some businesses in Indiana interpreted the law as allowing businesses they ran to stop serving LGBTQ people on the grounds that doing so would run counter to their religious beliefs.[1]

To make sure Kronites knew our company's stance, I wrote a message to employees expressing our concern about this law and confirming that although we "fully support freedom of religious beliefs," our company would "*always* treat every employee and every customer in a welcoming, respectful, and understanding manner, regardless of where they come from, how they worship, or who they love." I noted that this "has always been, and always will be, the Kronos way, and we will *never compromise* on these principles."

Political events aren't the only opportunities leaders and managers have to help employees feel safe. When natural disasters hit or other tragedies occur, employees also like to know that their employer stands behind them. In 2017, hurricanes Harvey and Irma were devastating. While the storm was still raging, I reached out with words of support. Many of our managers had been in continuous contact with their team members, and I publicly applauded them for this, affirming that this was "the level of care for each other that is at the heart of who we are as a company." I also let them know that we were hard at work tracking down all Kronites to make sure they were safe and arranging for appropriate care for those whose lives had been disrupted (see Chapter 7). Since we extend our emphasis on caring to customers, I told Kronites that we would be offering our customers free 24-hour support to help them weather the storms.

Beyond responding to major external crises, people managers should address developments inside the company that might cause anxiety or discomfort. Many employees worry about their job security. How well is the company performing? What does the outlook hold? Are any big organizational changes pending? Left unaddressed, these concerns can fester and affect engagement, even if a company is doing perfectly well and no major changes loom.

Mindful of Kronites' concerns, I provide updates on our performance, communicating financial data and describing opportunities as well as the challenges we face. I do this via e-mail, but also through impromptu aron@work videos I record on an iPad. In 2017, for instance, Kronites were concerned about the relocation of our headquarters to Lowell, Massachusetts, a city near our previous headquarters. Some employees weren't certain why we were moving, and they worried about what it might mean for their commute. To ease their concerns, I recorded an aron@work video with our chief procurement officer who was overseeing the move.

Occasionally, we have unpleasant company news to deliver, and in these situations, I go before Kronites and try to alleviate their fears as best I can. In 2009, when we were forced to let some Kronites go, those who remained were distraught and worried that they might be next. As I described in Chapter 2, I personally addressed employees, answering difficult questions directly and honestly, and explaining why it was economically necessary to reduce the size of our workforce. It took time for the organization to heal, but Kronites felt more secure knowing that our entire business wasn't falling apart, that we were responding rationally and thoughtfully to market trends, and that we had proceeded with staff reductions reluctantly, as a last resort.

You might wonder how far to take communication about external events and internal change. How much reassurance is too much? Should leaders and managers reach out in response to *every* external event or development that employees might find disturbing? Given how many storms, terrorist attacks, political controversies, and other bad news are reported on each week, the communications task would be endless.

I send financial updates about our company on a quarterly basis and sprinkle in additional messages throughout the year to highlight our strategies and major changes. Other senior leaders within Kronos communicate about changes in their respective departments, too. As far as external events are concerned, I am selective about which to respond to. I sent a companywide message of reassurance following the 2016 nightclub shooting in Orlando, Florida, but I didn't in response to other terrible terrorist attacks in the United States and other countries in which we operate. I responded to hurricanes Harvey and Irma, but not to hurricane Maria. I spoke up in response to immigration reform in 2017 but stayed silent on other controversial U.S. government policies.

I don't have a clear-cut rule on when to respond to external events, or when not to. I rely on my gut instinct. All of these tragedies affected me emotionally, but after certain of them I felt moved to say something to help reassure Kronites. Other times, it felt right to keep going with daily work and not intervene. It helps to think about the issues that are likely to concern your workforce, given their geographic location, demographic makeup, and so on. Using tactics described in Chapter 2, stay as close as possible to employees, conversing informally with them so that you can get an intuitive sense of their emotions. That way, when an external issue or development is bothering them, you'll be among the first to know.

There is no universal template, in my experience, for how best to craft a compelling message when you do choose to speak out. I can only offer advice based on what has worked for me. Speak honestly and authentically. If you work with a communications team like I do, don't let them script every word for you. It's *your* message. Use simple language and keep your message short and clear. At all times, remain mindful of employees and others who might disagree with you. Don't shrink from taking clear positions on controversial issues, but when you do take such positions, be respectful and civil. Don't let your own emotions overwhelm the message. The ultimate goal is to make your people feel safe. Finally, electronic communications are great, but there is nothing like face-to-face communication. If you lead a smaller team, and your teammates are all geographically proximate, gather everyone together and deliver your message in person.

BUILDING SAFETY AT THE ORGANIZATIONAL LEVEL

Personal communications from a leader or manager can go a long way to instill a sense of safety, but they aren't enough. If the organization doesn't back your words with action, your statements will seem hypocritical or superficial, and your efforts at leadership will backfire.

Diversity and inclusion is a good example. It's easy for me to circulate a message about Indiana's Religious Freedom Restoration Act because our policies welcome all people. We genuinely want all of our employees to bring their whole selves to work. To that end, we support and celebrate marriage, adoption, and childbirth for all employees. Likewise, while the technology industry has had its challenges welcoming women, we at Kronos fully accept them, not just as employees but as leaders. We support a Women's Leadership Forum to help women at Kronos network with one another and learn from each other's experiences. We work with the Society of Women Engineers to provide opportunities for women to advance their careers, and we support International Women's Day. I have also made a point of personally expressing my appreciation for the women in my life, as well as the valuable contributions made by female Kronites, through my aron@work video blog.

These programs and initiatives make an impact. In our 2017 employee engagement survey, 88 percent of Kronites agreed that we encourage and promote diversity of backgrounds, talents, and perspectives. That was far higher than the norm at technology companies, which stood at 68 percent. "I feel valued and appreciated each day at Kronos," one female Kronite wrote when responding to my 2017 International Women's Day video. After my 2016 election e-mail, an African American woman who worked at Kronos reported that she had "never—not one time— been made to feel inadequate or inferior to another individual within Kronos." In her view, she had been given "a chance to shine within this organization, regardless of my race, gender, or religious beliefs." That's exactly the kind of environment we want, a workplace where everyone can feel safe, and where they feel both grateful and inspired to do their very best.

Sometimes employees might feel unwelcome not because of some aspect of their identities but because they or their families might be struggling with difficult personal challenges. Here, too, organizations can take steps to help employees feel safe. In 2016, a Kronite was seeking help dealing with her daughter's addiction to opioids. The episode led us to create a training program to help other Kronites who have loved ones dealing with addiction. These employees might struggle alone, uncertain about whether to confide in colleagues. Our training program drew them out and established that they *could* talk about these issues at work and ask for support. As one employee told us, she and other Kronites "were suffering in silence until the program was launched. I had no idea I was working alongside so many people every day who were fighting the same battle." In Chapter 7, I noted that many Kronites think of our company as a big family. Here's another reason why: because even in dark times, they can still feel free to be themselves.

When it comes to easing Kronites' concerns about the health of the company and changes to our business, we find that engaging directly with employees and giving them a voice in the decision-making process goes a long way. It's one thing for me or another executive to personally assure Kronites that a given change won't pose a threat and is in everyone's best long-term interests, quite another for employees to have a hand in the decision-making process, and thus understand the nature of the change firsthand. As we prepared to move to a new headquarters in the city of Lowell, Massachusetts, we created a panel of employees—called our 5HIFT to Lowell Advocates—representing all functional areas within the company and charged the panel with helping leaders make key decisions about our new building. The panel received bimonthly briefings from the team overseeing the move and had a chance to weigh in. The panel offered numerous helpful insights and suggestions, and while many of them didn't weigh in on issues of physical safety per se, the ability to participate in decision making allowed these Kronites, and by extension the employees with whom they interacted back in their teams and departments, to feel more comfortable. Change was happening, but it wasn't coming out of nowhere, and it wasn't simply being imposed from above.

We also pay close attention to Kronites' need to feel safe and secure in their jobs when it comes to acquiring other companies. After acquiring more than 70 companies, we know that these transactions can trigger extreme anxiety in employees. Will the new company owners make changes to the business, letting employees go (which, unfortunately, we sometimes have to do when acquiring companies)? Will daily experiences at their workplaces be the same? Will the larger acquiring organization swallow up their company, leaving them feeling marginalized and unheard?

With such questions in mind, we take pains to assimilate acquired companies into Kronos with the least possible disruption for employees. A team of Kronites visits the acquired company, enthusiastically introducing employees to our culture. On the day we announce acquisitions, we meet with all new Kronites to explain the impact of the transaction on them and their jobs, having already closely researched the acquired workforce and the roles played by different teams there. We also train managers we've acquired in our culture, explaining how we think about managers at Kronos and giving them a wealth of tools and information. Recognizing how overwhelming it can be to receive large amounts of information at once, we conduct this training gradually, giving new managers time to adjust. To help new employees, we ask managers to share information about their team's integration into Kronos, sustaining the transparency that marks our culture. In the aftermath of the acquisition, we take additional steps to welcome the acquired company. For instance, I might mention it in a speech to hundreds of Kronites or customers. We'll also extend the same care to new employees that we do to all existing Kronites, offering assistance when a new employee is ill or suffers some other personal setback.

As newly acquired employees and managers tell us, these efforts make a big difference. Greg, whose company PDSI was acquired by Kronos in 2011, remembers how fearful his 65 employees were at first hearing the news. Many of them had heard from friends or relatives that acquisitions didn't go well, so they worried about their work-life balance, whether they'd be able to perform their jobs in the ways they were accustomed, and an array of other issues. Although some skeptical employees did not want to become Kronites (and wound up leaving Kronos), the vast majority made the transition thanks to our assimilation process. "We were embraced by all the [Kronos] teams we worked with. . . . We were welcomed. I mean, we were absolutely welcomed."

HUMAN LEADERSHIP

In January 2017, the U.S. presidential administration issued an executive order that prevented citizens of several Middle Eastern and Arab countries from entering the United States for 90 days. Many Kronites were concerned. Some 200 of our employees were in the United States on green cards, and almost half of those were staying on visas we had sponsored. Even if this executive order didn't affect them directly, would a subsequent order unsettle their lives? How vulnerable were they? Were immigrants from any country still welcome in the United States, and were they welcome at Kronos?

In the days immediately following, our human resources and legal teams helped relevant Kronites check on their immigration status and calm their fears. We also reviewed all employees around the world to see if anyone might be at risk of being denied entry into the United States. That way, we could intervene proactively and counsel employees about what to expect. We provided individual letters from our immigration attorney to Kronites traveling internationally, arming them in case they encountered problems at the border trying to reenter the United States.

Very soon thereafter, I sent a companywide note alerting Kronites to the support we were providing around immigration issues. I mentioned that we would continue to support *all* of our employees, irrespective of their background, and I asked Kronites to pursue this openness themselves and encourage others to do so. Finally, I reminded Kronites that some of their coworkers might be affected by the immigration issues, and so "may need an extra hug this week."

This message triggered a flurry of responses from Kronites. I wish I could quote them all because they so memorably evoke the power that leaders can have to help people feel safe and the immense gratitude you engender from employees when you do. A number of longtime Kronites wrote to say that it is messages like this one that help keep them happily employed with our company. As one said, "Having a leader who takes time out of their day to ensure that all employees feel safe, heard, and supported is absolutely amazing." Another Kronite said, "Thank you so much, from the bottom of my heart . . . this really means a lot to me."

Fostering engagement requires so much more than just making sure employees have the tools they need to succeed, are advancing their careers, and have meaningful work. It requires deep, personal engagement from leaders. And it requires taking care of employees' needs, even those that seem to extend beyond the confines of the workplace itself. In fact, *especially* those. Many companies get the "basics" of engagement right these days. But few treat employees as whole people, doing their best to take care of a range of emotional needs that can and do affect workplace performance. As leaders and managers, we have an incredible opportunity to make a difference in our employees' lives. We can teach them, coach them, and spur them to do great work, but we can also help them feel protected. When the rest of the world seems crazy, we can offer them an oasis of stability.

Be a human leader, one who helps create community. And help your organization be a more humane, protective space—especially in times of crisis, but at all other times, too. Your employees will never forget it.

9

Give Employees
Their Time Back

What would you do if your daughters were offered roles in a national touring theater production? Would you quit your job so you could spend months on the road with them? Would you have someone else accompany them? Or would you tell your daughters that they couldn't participate?

One of our employees, Kristen, might have faced this predicament had she worked at another company. In 2016, her two talented school-aged daughters were offered roles in the musical *Annie*. The tour would take place over eight months, stopping in over 90 cities throughout North America. The production company required that a parent or guardian accompany the girls. Kristen, who managed a small team at Kronos, wanted to accompany her kids on what would be a once-in-a-lifetime opportunity, but she wasn't sure what that would mean for her job.[1]

Kristen didn't have to worry because Kronos was among the few U.S. companies to offer employees open time off. In 2016, we implemented an open time off policy that featured no preset limit on how many days off employees can take. Employees and managers in the United States and Canada now work together to arrange as much vacation time as employees feel they need, so long as they achieve their individual and business goals. (In the future, we will consider rolling out this policy in additional countries, in accordance with local laws.) Called myTime, the program, along with our general commitment to flexibility, allowed Kristen to accompany her children on the *Annie* tour while still working full-time. She handled her Kronos responsibilities while her daughters were performing, communicating closely with her team about her schedule.

Many companies seem to want employees to prioritize their jobs above all else. To maximize performance, they try to keep employees in the office for as long as possible, providing all kinds of perks to make that kind of lifestyle possible and even attractive. At Kronos, 94 percent of employees surveyed in 2017 agreed with the statement: "I am able to take time off from work when I think it's necessary."[2] That's because we empower employees to put their families first, above the company. Our corporate values require this—and it's great for business. As we've observed, productive employees are, first and foremost, *engaged* employees. If you want to maintain high engagement levels, then you must empower workers to prioritize their families and bring their *whole* selves to work.

Because we enable Kronites to sustain their relationships at home, they come to work happier, treat their colleagues better, and perform better. They also express gratitude for such a nurturing and encouraging work environment, relieved that they aren't forced to choose between two vitally important parts of their lives—their careers and their personal relationships. One

Kronite whom I'll call Daniel used myTime to ride his motorcycle cross-country to raise money for multiple sclerosis research. In an e-mail, he expressed his deep loyalty to the company, writing: "Before I was financially invested . . . now you have my heart, too."

Commenting on her experience of being able to travel with her children, Kristen acknowledged the "great support" she received from Kronos, saying that her kids are "very aware just how lucky we are that I work for Kronos." They're not the only ones in luck. Our customers benefit, too, because they get the benefit of Kristen's and Daniel's passion and enthusiasm. Multiply that by the thousands of people who work at Kronos, and you understand how a "family-first" policy has helped propel our growth into a billion-dollar company.

MOVING TOWARD FLEXIBILITY

Our myTime program is hardly the first instance in which we've encouraged flexibility and healthy work-life balance among our employees. During the 1980s, when my brother Mark was CEO, our general counsel was a working mom. As Pat, our former president, remembers, when Sally went out for maternity leave, Mark personally worked with her to figure out a strategy for her return: "Mark said, 'Well, how do you want to work this? How many days can you work? We'll hire someone else to help you.'" I approached this the same way. When highly valued Kronites took leave to have children, we sat down together and created an arrangement that would make coming back to work palatable, sometimes opting for a three-day workweek, at other times allowing team members to work from home some days of the week. Back then, such flexibility was far from the norm, but we valued these employees' contributions and didn't want to lose them.

Since then, we've institutionalized flexibility by allowing Kronites to work remotely. Many of our employees work from home in some capacity, with the approval of their managers and if the nature of their job allows for it. We don't have a formal flexible time or work from home policy. Rather, we allow our managers to use their own discretion. If employees need flexibility around when their days begin or end, they can negotiate that with their managers. We've also invested in technological infrastructure to facilitate working remotely. In recent years, we started using an internal collaboration platform, as well as a unified communications platform that allows employees to access their Kronos phone line and voice mail from their mobile devices and laptops, no matter where in the world they might be. We even have an internal group on our social collaboration platform that's dedicated entirely to working remotely. Created by a Kronite who works out of her home, the group offers members advice for staying productive and connected.

With myTime, we've taken our longstanding commitment to flexibility and, as Pat (our former president mentioned previously) describes it, "put it on steroids."[3] Our approach emerged initially out of our desire to make ourselves more attractive as an employer. Back in 2014, we had hundreds of open positions and were having a really tough time filling them. If we didn't become more attractive to prospective Kronites, I felt we wouldn't be able to grow as I envisioned. One obstacle, it turned out, was our vacation policy. At the time, new Kronites received three weeks of paid vacation each year. Try enticing a veteran employee in her forties to come work for us when she was already receiving four or five weeks or more off elsewhere. Not easy! I asked our team to help me reimagine our vacation policies. After some research, they proposed that we adopt an open vacation policy. I liked it, as I saw instantly that it built on our longstanding "family-first" philosophy. I did my own research, and although I found instances in which companies had unsuccessfully dabbled with open time off policies, I felt confident that it would work for us. We decided to go ahead with myTime, hiring a consultant to help us avoid mistakes that other companies had made with similar policies.

We introduced myTime in 2016, and by all accounts it is a great success. I know of many Kronites who have used their increased flexibility to enhance their lives and their work performance. One of our employees used to save up all of her vacation time to visit her family in India every few years. That left her with no additional time off around the holidays to spend with her family in the United States. Now she can do both and still perform just as well, if not better. As validating as this story is, the data also suggests the value of myTime. In 2014, we were thrilled to discover that 84 percent of our employees thought we were a great employer. That placed us far above average in our industry, where roughly 60 percent of employees feel that way. So imagine our delight at learning that by the end of 2016, after a full year of myTime, our engagement score had risen to an exemplary 87 percent, and that employee turnover—already low compared to industry norms—was also down. A coincidence? I don't think so. Nor was it a coincidence that we had our best year ever financially in 2016.

After our experience launching myTime, I'm convinced that many companies can benefit from this kind of policy and from flexibility-oriented policies more generally. Here are some best practices based on our experience:

Build a Strong Culture First

One of the best things about myTime is that it is built organically on our preexisting company culture. As I described in Chapter 3, we've dedicated ourselves to nurturing an atmosphere at Kronos in which colleagues trust one another, assuming their competence and goodwill. We never could have succeeded with myTime if high levels of trust hadn't taken root in our organization. After all, in granting employees more latitude over their schedules, we were trusting them to do what it took to get their work done. Now, have some people abused the system? I'm sure they have. But any instances of people taking advantage, if any, have been few and minor. Kronites have again confirmed that our trust in them is warranted.

Our success with myTime also built on the work we've done to encourage open and honest communication between managers and employees. As we saw in Chapter 4, we train managers on how to communicate, and our Manager Effectiveness Index (MEI) both measures for it and promotes more conversation among teams. With myTime, our company was formally entrusting employees and managers to coordinate their scheduling needs. If we hadn't already developed expectations around communication, we couldn't necessarily count on the immediate success of myTime. Take an honest look at your culture. Does it have what you'll need to "give people their time back"? If not, try working on these fundamentals first and easing into more flexibility in the workplace before committing to a full-blown open vacation policy.

Keep Monitoring

Under traditional vacation policies, many companies rigorously track how much vacation employees have accrued and taken. In fact, our products help companies do precisely that. Were we undermining our own products? No! We still track vacation time, not to "keep an eye" on employees, but for the opposite reason: we want to make sure they are actually taking enough time off! We weren't just offering open time off to make ourselves look good: we truly believe that employees need this time for themselves and their families, and data shows that most Americans don't take as much vacation as they're allotted.[4] What good would our policy be if employees didn't take more time off? Happily, we've confirmed that Kronites are enjoying more vacation under our new policy: they took off an average of 2.6 more days in the first year of the program than they had the previous year. You'll also want to track engagement, recruitment, and other metrics to make sure your policy is working as intended.

Anticipate Bumps

As wonderful as myTime has been for us, the program's roll-out wasn't without its challenges. The vast majority of Kronites greeted myTime enthusiastically, but a small minority of people had reservations. Some managers worried that people would take advantage of the policy, or at the very least, that they'd be burdened with endless negotiations regarding employee requests for time off. Wouldn't it be simpler to have a clear policy? Some longtime employees were upset that they would no longer accrue unused vacation time and receive a bonus payout upon their retirement or when they left the company. And another group of Kronites felt it was unfair that everyone receives the same amount of vacation time. Why should an employee who had put in 20 years with the company receive as much time off as a 23-year-old newbie?

To ease our adoption of myTime, we addressed these concerns as best we could. We provided support to managers, coaching and training them on how to handle requests for time off and encouraging them to counsel their teams to take off more time, not less.

As for the other two concerns, we explained the policy to unhappy Kronites on a case-by-case basis. Look, I said to Kronites miffed at giving up their ability to accrue time off, do you think we give out vacation so that you can store it up? Not at all! We give it to you so that you can use it! I understood why these Kronites were upset, and I tried to acknowledge how they felt, but I made no excuses for the new policy. To Kronites who felt upset that myTime didn't reward their seniority, I tried to reframe the discussion, nudging them to dwell on the freedom the new policy afforded instead of focusing on others. Ultimately, I tried to recalibrate how everyone thought about vacation time. These Kronites were seeing it as a perk. We were treating it as something else: as a means of satisfying the need all employees have for a strong balance in their lives. That imperative outweighed other considerations.

Beyond opposition to myTime, some managers felt reluctant to give Kronites the time off they needed, fearing that it would hurt their businesses or bog their teams down with scheduling difficulties. In these situations, human resources stepped in, advising managers that we had to apply these policies equally where applicable or risk alienating individual employees. If that happened, managers' own MEI scores would decline. It was in everyone's interests to implement the new policy in an even and fair manner.

In the vast majority of organizations, flexible time off will represent a significant shift, so you can expect a certain amount of pushback. That's OK—be steadfast, and you'll reap the many benefits that Kronos has.

Be Clear About Your Motives

One reason many employees may distrust the idea of open time off is they regard it as a cost-cutting measure, a chance for companies to get out of paying for accrued vacation time when employees leave. Perhaps at some companies it has been, but that had never been our intention. To avoid any association of myTime with cost-cutting, we decided to do something no other company, to our knowledge, was doing: take the money we were saving by not paying departing employees accrued vacation times (about $2 to $3 million per year) and reinvest it in benefits for employees who *were* staying. We enhanced our 401(k) employer match and created a variety of enticing new programs. Kronos, on a selective basis, now offers college scholarships of $2,500 a year to children of our employees. We also offer student loan repayment assistance, childcare financial assistance, and adoption assistance, as well as a more generous parental leave benefit (maternity leave is fully covered for 12 weeks, and new dads and non–birth-giving moms can take a four-week paid leave, including for adoption). These new benefits enabled us simultaneously to build trust in myTime, further enhance our recruiting profile, and deepen our commitment to a "family-first" philosophy.

Kronites love these new benefits, and they especially love having open time off. Even many who resisted myTime at first now wholeheartedly embrace it. As one of our hourly workers wrote: "I can now attend to my personal business without 'guilt' or 'storing' days off, and trying to realistically coordinate scheduling too many appointments on a single day, or putting off important doctor's appointments because I wasn't able to coordinate [schedules]." The myTime policy did "take a little getting used to," this employee said, "but . . . with management cooperation, it has worked extremely well for me and my team. We actually communicate MORE now than we did in the past to ensure we have coverage for planned days out." On the whole, this employee "couldn't be happier with the flexibility and stress relief" myTime has afforded, and "definitely [counts myTime] as one of the biggest benefits" we offer. Not bad, right?

FAMILY-FRIENDLY LEADERS AND MANAGERS

As critical as flexibility around work-life balance is, you'll never truly empower employees to put family first unless you personally become involved as a leader or manager. Many employees today are used to working ridiculously hard, and to putting their families second. They might reasonably assume that their employers expect this level of commitment, even if companies move to open time off and affirm family's primacy. They might feel unsure about whether they really can miss an afternoon meeting to go to their kid's soccer game, circling back that evening to make up the work. Leaders and managers need to make a company's family-first philosophy *personal*, affirming and modeling it with their own words and actions.

For me, it feels natural to give such support because the notion of "family first" is deeply personal. I was privileged to grow up with parents who were unusually committed to family. They came to every one of our sporting events and school activities—no joke, every one! I appreciated it, and took the importance of family for granted. That said, I didn't always prioritize a healthy work-life balance for myself or my teams. When I was in my twenties and thirties, my work at Kronos *was* my life, and members of my team saw it the same way. We were mostly single and working in an intense start-up environment. Then, as mentioned earlier in this book, I had an encounter with a team member who expanded my horizons, pointing out that not everyone wanted to make their career at Kronos their entire life. That made an impression, and for years now, especially as I've had children of my own, I've more openly espoused how important it is to take time out and build strong personal relationships.

As Kronites will tell you, I talk about family *constantly*. When I chat casually with Kronites (Chapter 2), one of my first questions will usually be about their families. Lest employees think this is only talk, I try to set an example by prioritizing my own family. My daughters are grown now and out of the house, but when they were at home, I would do my best to attend as many of their after-school events as possible. "Mr. Ain," a girl on one of my daughter's sports teams once said, "how come you come to, like, all of our games?" I wasn't there at all of them, but I did attend most, and on many occasions, I was the only parent there. I would sometimes leave work at two in the afternoon, and when I did, I was sure to let my colleagues know where I was going. These days, I do my best to set limits and respect our family time. As CEO, I often can't help but make myself available on weekends and during vacations. Still, on a typical weekend, I will tune out of work on Friday evening, and stay away until sometime on Sunday, when I'll spend a number of hours catching up on work. Everyone's work-life needs are different. This pattern works for me, giving me the time I need to stay engaged with family while still putting my all into my work at Kronos.

I also promote a family-first culture by infusing my decision making with that philosophy whenever appropriate. In 2015, when we first realized that we needed a larger corporate headquarters, we asked a team of Kronites to investigate options. They returned with some suggestions in the Massachusetts towns of Burlington and Waltham. I said a quick no to those locations even though they would have resulted in a much shorter commute for me. We'd been at our location for 17 years. Kronites had made their lives in the area, buying homes and making decisions about their kids' schooling. If we moved to a site in the area that was 30 or 40 minutes away with traffic, we'd disrupt their home lives. They wouldn't be able to go to their kids' 5:30 p.m. softball games, like I had done. Our team eventually suggested a new location that was only three miles from where our offices were then situated. Pulling data, we determined that 83 percent of our employees would have a shorter commute to this new office. We went with that choice because it was better for the families of most Kronites.

THE FAMILY-FIRST CULTURE

At Kronos, employees expect that they'll have a life, and they encourage their colleagues to make the most of their family time as well. It's not that balancing work and home is easy at our company—not at all. Our people work *extremely* hard. They have their busy times when they absolutely must perform on behalf of customers, and they do. But the notion that a healthy work-life balance is doable, that you don't need to sacrifice one for the other, has become a company norm.

Respect for family has become so entrenched that it has changed new Kronites who joined us from other companies. One employee joined us midcareer and wound up working with the same boss she had had at a previous company. As this employee told us, her boss used to be quite rigid in his expectations. By 8:30 a.m., you had to be at your desk, and if you left your desk, you had to let your colleagues know. "Here," she said, "he's completely different," not as "uptight as he used to be. He's valuing his [own] family more than he used to . . ." Looking back on it, this employee attributed the change to working in the Kronos culture, and specifically to internalizing the example set by our leaders and managers.

All of our efforts have become a reason for our most valued employees to love their jobs, and hence, to stay with us, even though they have other options. It might seem counterintuitive, but no matter what kind of organization you run, or what size, you can energize and enthuse your workforce by enabling them to devote more energy at home. To convince you most fully of the merits of family-first policies, I'll leave you with the reflections of one Kronite: "Working from home is such a huge part of what makes working at Kronos so special," she says. "The ability to manage our workloads around our families and still deliver world-class services and products is quite amazing, and I would not give that up just for 'more money.'" This Kronite goes on to relate that she lives in Seattle, where "recruiters are constantly on the prowl for good talent. It has never before been so easy to turn down offers! The support we get, the remote work environment, the professional development, and the teams we belong to, all make working for Kronos worth so much more than just the money!"

For this Kronite, for the colleague of hers who responded with an "Amen, sister," and for many other employees with whom I've spoken, the power to put family first while still doing great work engenders true love for our company. Combine that with the other dimensions of a great job described in this book, and your people will be more engaged and dedicated to customers than ever before. I'm no Broadway star, but if you ask me, that really is something to sing about!

10

Welcome "Boomerang" Employees

In 2017, I received a message from a Kronite whom I'll call Ernie. A 25-year veteran of the company, Ernie had left about a year earlier to take a position at a global IT services firm. This firm had advertised Ernie's new job as a management role, but when he arrived, he was disappointed to find that it was actually a fairly junior consulting position that came with no management responsibilities. Still, he stuck around. Months later, another unpleasant surprise hit him. The company announced it was laying off thousands of employees. Since Ernie had the least seniority on his team, he was shown the door. Now Ernie was writing me to see if I could help him find a new position at Kronos.

Many leaders, upon receiving a message like this, might not have responded. Perceiving Ernie as disloyal for having left the company, they certainly wouldn't have welcomed him back into the organization. I was happy to help him, and I wrote him back that same day, telling him that I was forwarding his message to someone who would know about any job openings in his area of expertise.

At Kronos, we enthusiastically welcome back what we call "boomerang" employees, sometimes hiring them back just weeks after they've left. A Kronite, Brenda, wasn't happy with her "nasty commute" to and from work each day. She wondered what it would be like to work for a big consumer brand that she had long adored. With a bit of effort, she landed a job at this company in which she would do more or less what she had been doing for Kronos, with free sneakers and athletic wear to boot. She left for this opportunity. A few weeks later, she got back in touch with her Kronos manager. Her new job wasn't working out. The organization she had joined was disorganized, and as she told us, "The overall corporate culture was less than professional and too loosey-goosey for me." She asked for her old job back. Her manager said yes—without hesitation. She has been at Kronos for 18 years since.

Today, our hundreds of boomerang Kronites are among our most loyal and impassioned employees. Their stories are diverse and unique. One of our employees in India left because her husband transferred to a faraway city. An employee in Australia left because she wanted to experience the client side of our business. An employee in our Massachusetts headquarters left to start a business with a friend. Whatever their reasons, when these employees return, they bring with them a deeper appreciation of our culture, not least because they've seen what it's like in other workplaces. Brenda, the sneaker lover, told us that she has come to love how at Kronos, "all departments have a clear, concise mission" and departments "each work cohesively for a common goal—success and customer satisfaction."

Although more companies have come to welcome boomerangs (a 2017 survey of hiring and human resources managers found that almost 40 percent envisioned hiring former employees),[1] some people inside Kronos and other organizations still remain reluctant to rehire employees who've gone elsewhere, fearing that doing so would encourage more attrition among the existing workforce. Why would the company possibly want to send the message that it's OK to leave? I hate to see good people go as much as anyone, but I think our attitude toward boomerangs sends a much different message: That we're a confident company. That we care about our employees and want them to be happy. That we don't hold grudges. When other Kronites encounter boomerangs roaming the hallways, they're reminded of how unique an employer our company is. They're inspired to *stay*, not leave. Our stellar retention statistics are proof of that.

To build an energetic, inspired, high-performance workforce, have a more open mind to the topics of recruiting, development, and retention. In your capacity as a manager or leader, invest aggressively in developing your people, but don't hoard your talent and stigmatize employees for leaving. When former employees contact you about employment opportunities, do what you can to help them, up to and including hiring them back. They'll benefit—and so will your business.

LURING BACK BOOMERANGS

When I say we welcome back boomerangs, we don't simply respond favorably when former employees contact us, wanting to return. We actively recruit former employees. A Kronite—whom I'll call Kelly—who worked on our customer support team wanted to transition into a career as a software quality assurance engineer. After three years with us, she left to pursue training and to hone her skills at a smaller company. That company, a start-up, closed its doors shortly after Kelly had come on board, and a second company she joined laid her off after only about six months.

The day of the layoff, she was returning home when she heard the phone ringing. Guess who it was? A friend from Kronos, calling to see if Kelly would be willing to come back as a contractor in software quality assurance. No joke! Trying not to reveal her excitement, Kelly paused and said, "Sure, I guess I can do that." After the contract expired, she remained as a temporary Kronos employee until her manager decided that the team didn't have enough work to support her position. Unhappy to be leaving, she spent a few months looking for work. Then, as she says, "The unbelievable happened again." Kronos called with another temporary employment opportunity. This time, after a few weeks, she transitioned into a full-time position.

To Kelly, receiving a phone call from Kronos was "unbelievable," but we do this all the time—even contacting Kronites whom we've laid off. We also dedicate a page on our website to enticing boomerang employees to come back, announcing to them in big, bold lettering that "the door is open." We're so enthused about boomerangs, and so eager to position ourselves as a boomerang-friendly employer, that we've conducted independent research on the phenomenon. In 2015, our affiliated think tank, The Workforce Institute at Kronos, fielded an industry thought leadership survey of 1,800 employees, human resources professionals, and managers about attitudes toward boomerangs. As we found, managers were becoming more open to hiring former company employees, and employees were becoming more open to returning to firms where they'd formerly worked.[2] The survey generated widespread media interest, appearing in *Forbes*, the *Huffington Post*, and various blogs and industry publications.[3]

Now, we don't hire back every former Kronite who solicits employment. If employees have underperformed in the past, or if they've had trouble fitting into our culture, our hiring managers will typically pass. We also decline to extend offers if we don't have the right opportunities available. But if we do have those opportunities, and if former Kronites who were strong performers return to us seeking employment, we're quick to see if they might fill some of our open positions. From our point of view, these employees represent far less risk than new employees who have never worked for us. And we don't have to invest as much to train and onboard them. In our 2015 survey, a third of HR professionals and 38 percent of managers affirmed that "familiarity with the organization's culture is the biggest benefit to hiring back former employees, while nearly one-third appreciate that boomerangs do not require as much training as a brand-new employee."[4] Most of the time, we've found boomerangs can sign on and begin contributing to their teams much more quickly than ordinary new hires. It's a win for them, and for us.

YOU DON'T OWN YOUR EMPLOYEES' CAREERS

Skeptics might counter that boomerang employees actually do represent higher risk. Because they've left before, they stand a higher chance of leaving again. In the Kronos survey previously mentioned, almost one-third of managers and HR professionals subscribed to this belief, claiming that "boomerang employees have a stigma hanging over their heads."[5] I respectfully disagree. We haven't collected data on historical attrition rates among this group of employees, but we do know that while some do leave us again, the majority stay, often for years and even decades. They've seen what employment conditions are like at other companies, and they're even more appreciative of what they have at Kronos, especially our culture.

Even some employees whom we've had to let go in the past feel intense loyalty to Kronos once they've returned. John, who was laid off in 2001, came back to us four months later. As he told us, "Kronos was the first place to make me an offer while I was unemployed." He is still with us today. Another Kronite, also coincidentally named John, left Kronos when his department at Kronos dissolved. He worked elsewhere for five years. "I knew I was going to come back and work for this company again one day," he told us, "[and I am] very happy I did." He's been back for six years and loves his job. "Earning a living by keeping customers satisfied is what I enjoy doing," he said. He loves the teamwork and collaboration at Kronos.

Some laid-off Kronites do leave disgruntled, despite our best efforts to treat them compassionately. Some are so upset and resentful that they have little interest in returning. But it's remarkable—and inspiring—to see how many take such career setbacks in stride. Just as we've trusted them as employees, they trust that our decision to do away with their jobs wasn't personal, but rather something we had to do to secure the company's long-term health. As a result, they're often eager to return, if they can, and even more eager to stay once we've rehired them.

Even if boomerangs were less loyal than they've shown themselves to be, I would still feel perfectly comfortable rehiring them. It comes down to my personal philosophy underlying the employer-employee partnership. The way I see it, we as a company have a responsibility to invest in employees while they're working with us, developing their talent and helping them build their careers. And we do make that investment, offering a whole suite of employee development programs and initiatives, including on-the-job training and coaching, mentoring, functional rotations (in which high-potential Kronites can gain experience across the company), "Kronovation Days" that allow employees to work on projects outside of their ordinary jobs, "career matrices" that help employees understand the skills and experiences they need to progress in their careers, tuition reimbursement, and much more. These resources are so extensive that many Kronites cite them as reasons for their high engagement. As one remarked, "I am proud to be working for a company that encourages its employees to continue to learn and excel."

Despite our sizable investment, we don't feel entitled to total employee loyalty when it comes to career choices. As I like to say, *we don't own employees' careers.* We just don't. If people feel they need to leave our organization to pursue a dream, or take care of a sick relative, or make more money, or try out an opportunity that seems attractive in some other way, that's their prerogative. We don't—we can't—hold it against them. Think about how wrong it would be to do so. Individual employees only have one career. We, on the other hand, have thousands of employees. By definition, each employee's career will be more important to that Kronite than it is to the organization. We respect that and genuinely want our employees to make the career choices that best serve their own interests, even if it means that we occasionally lose some great people, as well as the investment we've made in developing them. When our best people leave and find success elsewhere, I am disappointed, but I understand it is likely the best career decision for them.

I should emphasize that this philosophy isn't just my own; most people managers at Kronos think this way. Quite frequently, our managers will spend years developing high-potential employees, only to find that their interests have changed and they want to explore opportunities elsewhere in the company. While our managers might feel disappointed to lose that talent on their team, they should never stand in the way of someone's career goals. One of our managers, who had recently helped two valued employees transition off her team into different functions inside the company, explains it this way: Her people "aren't going to be happy if they're here and looking to do something else. I'd want someone to do that for me." Another manager agreed, explaining: "It's really hard because inside you're screaming, 'I don't want to have to hire another person for this position.' But you're doing the right thing by these individuals."

As our managers also point out, setting employees free to pursue their careers is also a practical move. Employees who are held back and who have grown unhappy tend to spread their unhappiness to their teammates, causing overall engagement and morale to decline. "You just don't want the negativity," one manager said. On the other hand, another manager pointed to the intense loyalty that results when you develop employees and set them on a path they love, even if they wind up leaving your team. Describing a situation in which her best employee had just left on a six-month developmental assignment, a manager noted that her employee now "never wants to leave Kronos . . . I mean, she's like married to this company."

How do you as a manager think about your talent? Do you hold grudges when your best people leave? Do you want to cut ties, and do you resent their subsequent success? Are your organizational policies designed to retain people at all costs, dissuading them from pursuing career choices that might not serve the organization's short-term interest? Bottom line: you don't own their careers. They do. The sooner you accept and internalize that reality, the more affection and loyalty you'll garner. And the more likely you'll be to hire boomerangs, too—and reap the many rewards of doing so.

BENEFITS OF THE BOOMERANG

What are those rewards exactly, beyond loyalty, less risk to the company, and an easier time onboarding? Well, hiring boomerangs allows us to stay current with the realities of the modern workplace. You've heard statistics about how often millennials like to change jobs—I won't even bother repeating them. And you're no doubt aware of the gig economy phenomenon, whereby more and more workers shift between jobs and work multiple "gigs" simultaneously. Rehiring employees represents a tacit acknowledgment and acceptance of the fluidity that currently exists in the workforce. It positions us among job seekers as an employer in tune with the times, a company that "gets" the desire that many people feel to experiment with companies and to grow and evolve both personally and professionally.

Some of my favorite boomerang stories involve employees who left to experiment with other opportunities, including those that were largely unrelated to their work at Kronos. Paul, a project manager who had worked his way up to directing customer service for a geographic region, had long dreamed of working in film and television. In 2007, he had an opportunity to collaborate on some short films and TV shows. Although the money was unsteady, he embraced the opportunity, supplementing his income by designing apps in his spare time. He returned to Kronos after the birth of his son, realizing that while TV and film work was fun, he "needed something that could be fulfilling *and* stable." Seven years later, he remains at Kronos. As he remarks, "Kronos's culture of taking care of employees and insisting on [not paying lip service to] having a work/home life balance makes it the perfect place to work with new technology, while still making the time to be daddy to my little boy."

Another Kronite, Sandy, joined us in 1989 and worked her way up to manage one of our large corporate accounts. In 2002, she "still had a few dreams to pursue," so she left, enrolled in culinary school, became a chef, and opened a small catering company. Several years later, she wanted to return to a more corporate environment, so she took a position with a consulting firm that partners with Kronos. Three months after that, she "crossed back over" to become a Kronos employee.

As these stories suggest, our approach to boomerangs strengthen our culture, affirming that we care for employees and their careers. Many boomerangs leave Kronos not because they want to, but because their families need them. A Kronite—whom I'll call Scott—had a family member with special needs, and he found it hard to travel for his job at Kronos. He felt Kronos couldn't accommodate his need to restrict travel, so he left and took a position with another company. Three months later, his former boss at Kronos contacted him with news that his team could now accommodate his need for reduced travel, so he eagerly returned. Another employee, Laura, left to stay at home full-time with her two young children, returning 14 years later when her kids were older and more independent. If Kronos shut the door on such employees, we'd be contradicting our family-first philosophy. By welcoming them back, we generate more trust and affection among boomerangs and their colleagues alike.

A final reason to welcome back boomerangs is to benefit from the considerable knowledge and experience they gain while working elsewhere. Many boomerangs leave to join start-ups. Upon their return, they contribute entrepreneurial energy and excitement to their teams, furthering our own efforts in this area (Chapter 13). Some go to work on the client side of our business, and when they return, help to inject a deeper understanding of the client perspective into our teams. Still others are exposed to new technologies or industries and bring that knowledge back to the company. Of course, any new employee will contribute new knowledge, perspectives, and ideas. But since boomerangs also are already deeply embedded in our culture, we get the best of both worlds: veteran employees who nonetheless can freshen our culture and expand our horizons.

THE ULTIMATE BOOMERANG

In the summer of 2014, I heard a knock on my office door. Dave, our chief people officer, wanted to speak with me. I assumed it was about one of our policies, or perhaps a new idea for continuing to build our culture and increase engagement. I was in for quite a surprise. A much larger company had offered him a job. The compensation package was extraordinary, far above market value for someone in his position, and certainly far more than Kronos could match.

I shook my head. Dave had played a key role in helping me execute my vision of providing a highly inspiring and engaging workplace. I didn't want to see him go, but at the same time, I knew this opportunity would be wonderful for him and his family. Frankly, I didn't see how he could turn it down, and I told him so.

Dave and I continued to discuss his situation. I was a bit suspicious about why this new company was offering such high compensation. I wondered if something was going on behind the scenes that they weren't telling him. Dave agreed, but he wasn't terribly concerned. In his mind, the offer was incredibly attractive. In the end, he decided to take the new job. As we said our goodbyes, I told him to remember Kronos after he started his new job. I told him that if he was unsure about his decision, he should imagine that a little birdie was sitting on his shoulder, chirping, "My previous job at Kronos is not going to be open forever!"

A couple of days after he started his new job, I called him with the news that the *Boston Globe* had named us the best place to work among large companies in the state of Massachusetts. I kidded around with him, saying, "I don't know why you'd want to work someplace else, when you already worked at the best place to work." A few weeks after that, Dave called and asked if we could grab a coffee. I assumed he wanted my permission to recruit members of his former Kronos team for his new company, and I was prepared to be furious with him. In my head, I had composed a whole tirade about how inappropriate that was. But when he came in, Dave told me that while the money was great, the new job wasn't in line with what he expected. He wanted to know: could he come back home to Kronos?

Uh, yes! Right then and there, I called our board chairman to discuss the logistics of bringing Dave back as a boomerang. Within 10 minutes, we had an agreement. Dave was coming back.

I didn't begrudge Dave for leaving. If anything, the episode left us even more committed to our policy of respecting people's careers and welcoming back boomerangs. I mean, come on, even our chief people officer, the person charged with helping us retain our best employees, is a boomerang!

Even prior to Dave's return, boomerangs gave rise to a kind of subculture within Kronos. You heard chatter about boomerangs at meetings, in the hallways, on the elevator. Always, this chatter was accompanied by expressions of affection for Kronos. Employees took pride in identifying themselves as boomerangs.

Dave continued this tradition. Not long after his return, a few of his colleagues welcomed him back by playfully presenting him with an actual wooden boomerang, with an inscribed handwritten message, "Welcome back to the 'Ultimate Boomer-ang!'" That gift still hangs in Dave's office, a testament to the importance of empowering employees to live their lives and pursue their dreams, wherever that might take them.

11

Celebrate to Motivate

It was January 2018, and I was standing on a stage at a beautiful resort in Cancun, Mexico. Sitting in the audience were 200 of our sales and services people, along with 150 of their guests. We were all there on our annual Legend Makers trip, intended to reward top-performing Kronites for their efforts. One highlight of the trip is the awards banquet, at which we present a series of long-term Milestone awards recognizing employees who have earned the Legend Makers trip multiple times.

At events like these, senior leaders often recognize high-achieving individuals, shake their hands, and say some words of thanks. On this evening, I went further and asked each Kronite who was celebrating 15 years as a Legend Maker award winner to join me on stage one at a time in front of all attendees. I spent a few minutes with each of them, reviewing highlights of his or her career—my memories of significant customer wins, how he or she went above and beyond for customers, and so on. During this personal exchange, I also explained the impact that the individual employee had achieved at Kronos.

One Kronite, Jay, confessed upon coming to the stage that he was worried he looked older up there. I joked around with him, telling him that he looked the same as when I first met him. Then I got down to business. Reminding everyone that Jay was a boomerang, I told him that "everything you've ever done at Kronos has been remarkable," including opening up new territories and selling our biggest accounts and newest products. I recognized his "endless courage, commitment, focus," and the "magical way [he had] of getting other people to feel great about working with you, and they want to help you, and they want to be part of your team, and they want to be successful with you, and they want to be around you," and that included me. On an even more personal note, I also told him that I admired how he looked out for his parents, his wife, Jill, and his boys, and that he was a beacon at Kronos for the extraordinary dedication he showed to his family. I closed by recounting a story of how he persevered with a prospective client, working for months before closing a multimillion-dollar deal for us with a major hotel brand.

After Jay left the stage, I called up Peter, who runs our Australian operations. I recounted how we'd met 19 years prior in Sydney, and how he'd transformed a small operation into a leader in Australia and New Zealand. I recognized his immense professional courage, and his ability to build a special team. "You spend as much time telling me how your people are doing as you do telling me how *you're* doing," I said. "You get more pride in the success of your team members than your own success." I told him that this is why his team is so devoted to him—because he'd do anything for them. "I want to thank you," I said. "You know how I feel about you, how special you are to me," and that we "would not be the company we are" without his efforts.

After these presentations, we adjourned for dinner. As I circulated among the Legend Maker winners and their invited guests, I found that many people in the room were astonished that the CEO of a global company knew so much about a sales or service person and could speak about him or her with such familiarity and passion. "I've never seen anything like that," people said to me afterward. I thought, "Wow. Never? That's a shame."

As I've learned over my career, it's *critical* to recognize people for their professional accomplishments and personal milestones. It goes to the core of performance. Employees appreciate recognition from others, and they're more motivated to perform when they receive it. As one of our Legend Maker recipients put it, the event is motivating because "you're at a spectacular resort, you're hanging out with the best of the best in the company, and it makes you really feel good that you're at the top echelon of your peers." Do you suppose this Kronite would return from a Legend Makers trip feeling only so-so about his job and our company? Of course not!

Conversely, when employees don't receive recognition, they become demotivated and begin seeking work elsewhere. In 2015, our corporate think tank, The Workforce Institute at Kronos, polled 855 U.S. employees, asking them questions about the factors that led to their day-to-day happiness on the job. The industry thought leadership survey found a direct correlation between employees who felt underappreciated and those actively looking for a new job. Of the 61 percent of respondents who said that they had thought about looking for a new job within the past 12 months, a majority—59 percent—felt either unappreciated or only somewhat appreciated at work. A mere 11 percent felt strongly appreciated.[1]

Many organizations and teams have programs in place to reward outstanding performance, offering trips, bonuses, and the like. Yet these standard programs might not go far enough, especially when leaders don't become personally involved in extending recognition and gratitude. As our industry survey found, 50 percent of employees either didn't feel appreciated or felt only a little appreciated. Over 40 percent reported that their company was only "average" in the appreciation it showed to employees, and a good slice of respondents—20 percent—said their company was "one of the worst" in this area.

Is employee recognition lackluster or an afterthought in your organization? If you're a manager, is thanking and celebrating team members something you do as a matter of course, rather than a focus of real enthusiasm, creativity, and innovation? To build engagement and enhance performance, managers have to make legends out of their most deserving employees, and organizations must create an array of formal mechanisms to recognize the greatness of individual employees and to mark turning points in their lives. It's about creating a *culture* of gratitude and acknowledgment. Your organization has extraordinary contributors working for it, and you have so much to gain by taking notice and celebrating them.

SIX TECHNIQUES FOR SAYING "THANK YOU"

In recent years, as we've worked on building our WorkInspired culture, we've updated and enhanced our corporate programs recognizing and rewarding great performance. Employees now single them out as a reason why they love working at our organization. But why keep them a secret? Companies of any size and sector can use the following strategies to foster a strong, creative, and enduring culture of employee celebration.

Create Forums for Employees to Thank One Another

One Friday morning in 2017, shortly before her team relocated to our new headquarters in Lowell, Massachusetts, one of our employees, Melissa, stopped by the new offices to take a look. She was blown away by how beautiful and functional the space was, and felt moved to say thanks to the dozens of Kronites who in one way or another had helped design and outfit the new headquarters. In many organizations of any size, it's difficult for employees to express public gratitude—there isn't a forum for it. For Melissa, though, it was easy: just jump on our internal collaboration platform, and write a post. "I just wanted to share some thoughts and give kudos to all involved in our 5HIFT to Lowell," Melissa wrote. "I am utterly impressed with how much thought went into the design." Others posted comments affirming her sentiments, with one writing: "Love this enthusiasm on a Friday!"

Gratitude shouldn't just flow from the top of the organization down, but horizontally as well. In our 2015 Workforce Institute study, over two-thirds of respondents told us that they felt a sense of satisfaction when fielding positive feedback from other employees.

Kronites thank one another all the time on our collaboration tool, and they have also used 5HIFT Shout-Outs, a global peer-to-peer recognition program that allows employees to acknowledge the efforts of colleagues cross-functionally and in any region. We unrolled Shout-Outs as part of our continued efforts to become a software-as-a-service (SaaS) company. All Kronites have the unlimited opportunity to recognize colleagues for one of our five "5HIFT Behaviors" we needed to see for our SaaS transformation to succeed: "customer first, humility, empowerment, collaboration, and courage."[2] Kronites fill out a brief online form, describing the employee and the behavior they want to recognize, and the company sends a congratulatory thank-you e-mail to the Shout-Out recipient and his or her manager. The recipient's name also appears on our Make the 5HIFT site for all Kronites to see, and we enter him or her as well as the name of the Shout-Out nominator into a monthly drawing to receive a gift card. At the end of the year, we select three grand prize winners from among Shout-Out nominators and recipients to receive weekend getaways of their choosing.

It didn't take long for the program to catch on. To keep senior leaders updated on the program's impact, we send them monthly data dashboards. During the program's first year, Kronites sent over 5,000 Shout-Outs. As one Kronite told us, "Of all the recognition programs I've seen, this one is my favorite—simple and effective!" A manager told us that Shout-Outs were a "good way to reach out to people [who] might be remote or [whom] you might have never met before, but [who] helped you out big time with something little or at the last minute."

Allow Teams, Departments, and Business Units to Offer Their Own Recognition

Several departments layered their own Shout-Out programs on top of our corporate contest, giving Kronites within their team extra opportunities for recognition and rewards. Marketing, for instance, ran separate cash raffles at each of its quarterly update meetings for employees who gave or received Shout-Outs during the quarter. Two other departments within Kronos ran monthly recognition programs, while one department ran a weekly Shout-Out program. These programs recognized Kronites for meaningful contributions they made in the course of their daily work. One particular Kronite received a Shout-Out for collaborating on a customer issue after hours, staying on the phone with the customer for more than two hours. Another Kronite received one for being the "point person" for a unit's move to our new headquarters, working diligently to ensure that the move went smoothly.

Corporate doesn't have to "own" recognition. Rather, it can serve as an instigator and promoter of other grassroots recognition programs that spontaneously develop across the organization. Leaders should also encourage departments and teams to develop their own internal awards programs tailored to their discrete goals and initiatives. Our finance department, for instance, publicly recognizes a number of team members at the end of its quarterly meetings for exemplifying our core competencies of character, competence, and collaboration, with each winner receiving a bonus. Our product, technology, and cloud group has pursued a manager-to-employee recognition program called High Five. Managers recognize achievement during the work week, handing out High Five chips as well as verbal recognition. Once an employee receives a chip, he or she is added to an online ranking board. At the end of the year, team members who have amassed the most chips receive rewards.

With both corporate and team or department programs in place, Kronites can be recognized multiple times in the same quarterly cycle, and that recognition can come from multiple sources. The way we see it, the more recognition, the better!

Provide Special Opportunities for Employees to Thank Their Managers

Many organizations don't think to publicly celebrate successful managers the way they might celebrate their top sales leaders. But we do. As I related in Chapter 4, we believe that every Kronite deserves a great manager, and we have invested in management development across the organization through our Courage to

Lead training program. Perceiving celebration to be an important and necessary part of this investment, we created a Courage to Lead Award program to recognize outstanding managers. All managers at Kronos are eligible, with nominations coming directly from employees via an online portal. Each year, our executive committee selects up to 25 winners from among our approximately 800 people managers, bringing them to Boston near our corporate headquarters for a special awards ceremony, and giving each recipient a vacation getaway. After the awards ceremony, we further promote the year's Courage to Lead winners in various ways.

Besides motivating managers to improve, a formal program that enables employees to thank their managers accomplishes a number of important objectives at once. It injects gratitude into our culture and sends a message about how much we value and support managers. It also enables us to highlight the specific manager behaviors we're trying to encourage. Perhaps most important, it gives employees a voice, affirming the notion that our leadership team is listening directly to them, and that they can help build the culture that they want.

Provide Public Recognition, Not Just Rewards

Kronites like receiving gift cards and other rewards—who doesn't? But pure public recognition goes a long way, too.

A member of our legal team, Lauren, began in our marketing department but had always dreamed of becoming a lawyer, so she went to law school at night while continuing to work for us full time. Our legal team heard that Lauren had enrolled as a law student, and began discussing her studies with her in the hallway. Over time, friendships grew. When Lauren graduated, we happened to have an opening in our legal department, and jumped to hire her. Lauren was thrilled, as it was difficult for newly minted attorneys to find a job as a corporate counsel without having put in years first at outside law firms. Today, Lauren helps us with customer contracts, applying the knowledge about our sales process she's gained from her earlier marketing work.

One of Lauren's colleagues found her story so inspiring that she nominated Lauren to be profiled on "Career Spotlight," a special feature we produce that profiles Kronites and their career stories. Any Kronite at any level can nominate a fellow employee. Our communications team then interviews the person nominating the employee, the nominee, and the nominee's manager and writes an inspiring story. This recognition not only raises the profile of the featured Kronite within the organization, but also promotes our culture of caring. Further, the profiles provide examples of professional and personal growth that serve as road maps for younger Kronites contemplating their career direction.

Lauren's profile ran under the headline "Attorney at Law, Chaser of Dreams." Other Kronites were so inspired by her story that they posted comments on our internal collaboration platform, where we promoted the profile, to congratulate her on the recognition and all she had accomplished. "[Lauren] is an inspiration to me," one wrote. "She is fiercely intelligent and driven—and at the same time a great teammate. I am thrilled that she has been able to realize her dream while remaining part of the Kronos family." Imagine how valued Lauren must have felt to have been validated in this way not just by the organization but by her colleagues.

Recognize Your People for Referring New Employees

Many companies offer bonuses or other incentives to employees for helping the organization recruit new talent. For years, we gave out cash rewards when we hired employee referrals. In 2016, we revamped this program to maximize its impact. Whenever a Kronite refers a potential hire, we enter him or her into a quarterly drawing, giving him or her a chance to win merchandise from our company store. If we hire the referral, the referring Kronite receives a cash reward. At the end of the year, we enter all hired referrals and Kronites who referred them into a Hiring Hero Recognition drawing. The winning duo (a new hire and the Kronite who referred him or her) can choose more items from our store. Significantly, this program rewards and acknowledges all Kronite referrals equally (we used to pay more of a bonus for people hired into senior level positions). This feature reflects our belief that great businesses are powered by great people at every level, and that we as a company should care for all people equally.

Practice Mass Gratitude

Another tactic we deploy is to hold events that allow us to express gratitude to large groups of Kronites all at once. Each summer, more than 1,500 Kronites at our corporate headquarters take an afternoon off from work to attend an employee appreciation picnic. It's an enormous BBQ extravaganza, with music, carnival games, volleyball, corn hole toss, and a basketball tournament. Departments often plan team meetings around the picnic, too, so Kronites from other regions can attend while visiting our headquarters. In 2017, we introduced a new event, the Souper Bowl, in which Kronites make chili or soup for their colleagues to try. Each Kronite paid a five-dollar fee (to taste the culinary creations), which we donated to a local food pantry. We have also historically held a Thanksgiving luncheon in November during which our executive team, including me, dons chef coats and hats to serve lunch to employees at our corporate headquarters. We likewise encourage our regional offices to host their own similar events. Many companies have events such as these, but if yours doesn't, or if your events are lackluster and uninspiring, I would suggest making an investment here. As we've found, these events are wonderful opportunities not merely to show gratitude and affirm it as one of our key values, but also to support strong bonds among our employees, a sense that we're all one big family.

THE SEVENTH TECHNIQUE: GRATITUDE FROM THE TOP

As important as these programs are individually, their biggest contribution is to create a greater culture of recognition, in which expressing gratitude at all levels becomes the norm, and everyone feels empowered to say, "Thank you." As our research has shown, personal expressions of recognition or gratitude from bosses and fellow colleagues mean the most to employees. In our 2015 Workforce Institute poll, 55 percent of respondents reported that having a direct boss thank them left them feeling highly satisfied with their jobs, as compared with only 28 percent who said the same of receiving public recognition from their organization. Respondents preferred to receive thanks from their boss privately, rather than with others present, and in person rather than via electronic means.

As a leader or manager, make a practice of expressing personal gratitude whenever you can. If your team, department, or organization has formal recognition programs in place, maximize your personal engagement and presence. As Mike, one of our Legend Maker winners, said, "It's a humbling experience to be up in front of all of your peers and [to get] your award from

Aron [and other leaders]." Don't wait for formal award ceremonies to extend your thanks. Look for opportunities to do so in the
course of your daily work. Often, it's just a matter of taking a little extra time. When the manager who helped launch our India
operations marked 10 years of employment with us, I wrote him
a personal e-mail in which I recalled all he had accomplished.

Likewise, when we provide software to a new customer, we
conduct "milestone" surveys over the phone at a certain point
in the process to gauge overall experience and general satisfaction with our products and services. I review the results, and
whenever I see that customers have given our teams the highest
possible rating, I typically send a personal e-mail to employees
on the project, acknowledging their great work and thanking
them for it. This kind of recognition—in fact, any recognition
from outside a Kronite's team—helps people feel valued. As one
of our business unit managers remarked, "I know that when my
team gets recognition from outside, they're like, 'Wow, the business noticed.' And that goes a long way."

In virtually every speech I give to Kronites, I thank them for
all the hard work they do to make our company successful. When
I walk through our hallways chatting informally with Kronites,
I often thank people for their efforts and commitment. And as I
mentioned in Chapter 1, I make a point of giving Kronites credit
in meetings, especially junior Kronites. As a member of our executive team noted, doing that allows everyone to leave "feeling
like a big deal." That's as it should be—because at Kronos, everyone *is* a big deal. Everyone contributes to our success.

In line with our family-first philosophy, I also make sure to
thank the family members of Kronites in speeches and on other
occasions. As I tell people, "Go home and hug your loved ones
and thank them. Because they allow you to put in the effort you
do, that in turn helps make Kronos great."

THE POWER OF "THANK YOU"

When I attend Legend Makers and bring onstage veteran Kronites to receive my personal thanks, I notice something interesting. Some of the individuals we're honoring revel in the experience. They might be nervous standing up there in front of hundreds of people, including their invited guest, but their faces shine with great pride. They bask in the recognition—it's a high point of their career. Other winners take less pleasure in the experience. The honor we're bestowing is immensely meaningful to them, but some feel embarrassed by my public recounting of all that they have accomplished and how much the organization and I value them.

It doesn't matter what kind of personality you have, or whether specific individuals on your team relish public recognition or not. As a manager who is striving to build an engaged workforce, you have to publicly recognize your people. It's that important. Some managers may think that salary increases and promotions boost motivation. What matters for the vast majority of people is the appreciation you personally show. People look to the person in charge for guidance, assistance, affirmation, and yes, appreciation. They want to feel *valued*. And you, more than anyone else, can provide that. Isn't that incredible? You have the power to make someone feel great about themselves and their work.

Our organizations, too, have this power, albeit to a lesser extent, and they need to use it. If your organization isn't prepared to recognize, acknowledge, and cheer your teams and individual employees, your workforce won't be as engaged as it could otherwise be, and your organization won't be as successful. I've seen this connection at play year after year. As one Kronite stated, "Kronos has proven to be very concerned with recognizing and rewarding the people who make exceptional contributions. This makes Kronos a very satisfying place to work and helps individuals to feel appreciated." Employees will love where they work when you express love for them. And a great place to start is by saying a simple "Thank you."

Respect
Everyone's Culture

In India, companies don't just hold ribbon-cutting ceremonies when opening new offices or starting new ventures. They also hold Puja ceremonies, in which a Hindu priest asks for the divine blessings of Lord Ganesha, Goddess Lakshmi, and all planets. The proceedings, which can take multiple hours, include the lighting of candles, chanting, the recitation of Sanskrit hymns, and a number of other rituals. I know because in 2009, I had the honor of traveling to Bangalore and participating in a Puja ceremony to mark the opening of a new Kronos office in India. With other Kronites in attendance, a priest in a white robe draped garlands of white flowers around my neck while reciting a prayer. I lit a golden ceremonial lamp and, with a dot of red in the middle of my forehead (a bindi, it's called), joined assembled executives and employees in prayer.

I had never done anything like this in my life, and I was humbled by it—also a bit nervous. Fearing that I would somehow make a mistake, I did everything the priest asked. When I didn't understand something, I peppered James, one of the leaders of our India operation, with questions. "It's extremely important for a large number of employees that the gods are invoked as per Hindu traditions," James says. "Seeing their American CEO so keen to be an active participant in the rituals made a big impression and gave our early employees a sense of personal connection." But it was more than that. Our India employees had taken a risk in signing on with Kronos. Our brand was unknown in the India market, and our business of workforce management was also largely unfamiliar. By taking part in the Puja ceremony, I helped employees feel more comfortable with Kronos. Seeing that I was doing my utmost to understand their religious rituals, they felt more confident that our leadership team would respect the uniqueness of the India market and give them a measure of autonomy, rather than imposing decisions from our headquarters.

Some people wonder whether companies can remain amazing places to work as they expand their footprints. Can companies sustain high engagement when their workforce becomes more diverse and geographically dispersed? Don't these employees have disparate needs, and doesn't growth dilute the original culture?

Growth doesn't have to come at the cost of engagement— quite the contrary. Over the past decade, we've pursued a strategy of aggressive global expansion, hiring Kronites or signing on partners throughout the world. Our business has performed better in some countries than in others, but across the board we've sought to spread our WorkInspired culture to create environments in which employees love to work. To date, we've won "Best

Place to Work" awards in Australia, Canada, China, India, the United Kingdom, and the United States. Also, our engagement scores in virtually every country run above the country average, and in some cases far above. In 2017, 95 percent of our Australia workforce was positively engaged, compared with a 2016 national average of only 63 percent. Our China workforce reported a 90 percent engagement level, much better than the national average of 66 percent. Levels like these establish our organization as a premier employer, making recruiting and retention easier and less expensive. They enable us to serve our customers better and to innovate more readily. In almost every respect, they make us more competitive.

How did we do it? It comes down to respecting everyone's culture. As CEO, I make a personal effort to participate in local cultural traditions and to communicate in culturally sensitive ways. Meanwhile, we consciously extend our culture to all Kronites, regardless of who they are and where they work. We've discovered that people of different cultures bring a rich tapestry of ideas and norms to the workplace. Celebrating these cultures and letting people be themselves opens up a wealth of opportunities, and it certainly makes work more fun and interesting.

If the organization you lead is embarking on a global strategy, or if you've been assigned to manage a global team, I urge you to open your heart and cultivate a posture of flexibility and open-mindedness. It's unbelievably enjoyable to do, and it helps the business. Rather than assuming you always know best, listen to the needs and desires of employees around the world, and adapt your practices and policies accordingly. Reach out to employees, regardless of where they work, soliciting feedback and taking meaningful action. Send a message that all employees matter, and that the organization is committed to respecting differences and empowering everyone to succeed. By remaining open-minded and by parting with the idea that the entire world revolves around us and our norms, our companies and teams can make the most of our diverse workforces.

WORKINSPIRED IS GLOBAL-READY

It's easy to talk about openness and cultural sensitivity, but quite another task to put these values into practice. The good news is that if you embrace the principles, organizational policies, and leadership practices we've examined so far in this book, you're already moving in the right direction. In our experience, WorkInspired by its very nature encourages Kronites to treat colleagues around the world with respect, and to maintain an attitude of flexibility and curiosity. In this way, WorkInspired has made Kronos "global-ready," giving us a head start on integrating all personnel into our organization and helping us to foster strong engagement worldwide. It has also positioned our leaders to inspire and motivate people across geographic divides through our own behavior.

Take the principle of trust. I've described how we empower employees by explicitly encouraging leaders and managers to trust their people. Rather than micromanaging, we assume competence and give Kronites latitude to exercise their own judgment. Translated into a global context, that principle leads me and others at Kronos to give our people, regardless of where they reside, a great deal of autonomy. As a general rule, I'm happy if our regional or division leaders consult me on business decisions, but I don't interfere. In fact, when our corporate processes impede our local teams, I will encourage them to engineer their own solutions to pressing business issues. If our corporate training programs aren't giving employees in China or India the skills they need, our regional leaders can devise and implement their own training because we trust their judgment. If certain human resources policies aren't appropriate for a particular market, we'll adjust accordingly. Because of this flexibility, Kronites around the world feel more valued and empowered. As Jaime, head of marketing for Latin America, says, "We feel we have the power to manage our challenges and make decisions immediately."

Another element of our culture's emphasis on caring for people and helping them to feel safe also leads us to welcome Kronites around the world and forge emotional bonds with them. I've described the e-mail I wrote in the wake of the 2016 U.S. presidential election to reassure Kronites that our company would "always provide a caring environment that is supportive and encouraging," and that we would "be fully supportive of our employees of all backgrounds, faiths, and genders, no matter where they live, who they love, or where they worship." In that e-mail, I also took the opportunity to specifically reassure certain of our global employees, writing, "For our cherished staff in China and Mexico, I want to state clearly that you are an important part of our organization, and we will continue to invest in our operations in these regions to grow and support our staff, customers, and partners. This same standard applies to ALL Kronites around the world. We will set our own pace, make our own decisions, and choose the way we do business that creates positivity and unification of spirit and purpose."

Among the hundreds of responses I received from Kronites, many came from employees outside the United States. They were astonished and reassured that their CEO would take such a firm stance on behalf of inclusion. One of our Mexico employees wrote: "Your words give me confidence to keep on working as always, with great enthusiasm day by day with the great team we have in Mexico. From my heart, thank you very much." I didn't conceive this e-mail specifically with our global employees in mind, but because I sent it and because I took care to mention them specifically, I was able to nurture their loyalty and engagement. They perceived that our culture of safety extended to *them,* even though they spoke a different language and worked in another country.

Our culture produced a similar outcome in the wake of the 2017 earthquake in Mexico. Immediately after the quake struck, teams at our corporate headquarters spent hours checking on our Mexico colleagues. We learned that homes had been damaged, and public transportation in Mexico City was extremely limited, so our corporate team booked hotel rooms near the office as a precaution. We launched our Emergency Management Notification System, sending out a polling text message that asked employees in Mexico if they were safe. Fortunately, we were soon able to account for all of our employees. The next day, engineers inspected our building in Mexico City and determined that it was safe.

Four years earlier, our leaders in Mexico had asked for funding to relocate to a new office building, in part because they needed more space, but also because the existing building wasn't constructed in compliance with current earthquake regulations. Our corporate leadership worked with our leaders in Mexico to find new offices in a modern, seismically ready building. These efforts and our swift actions made them feel respected and cared for. "We feel that the company is very human," said Jaime. "And [that] the most important [concern of Kronos] is our people." We'd listened to the needs of Kronites abroad and seen to their safety—not because of some special corporate initiative or strategy, but because WorkInspired implicitly tells us to do so.

Overcommunication, another principle within our culture, also helps us welcome our global workforce. I've mentioned my habit of kibitzing (engaging in informal conversations) with Kronites. I do this with our leaders throughout the world. When I visit our overseas locations, I spend time beforehand reviewing who works in that particular region. When I arrive, I try to shake hands and say hello to every Kronite, remembering their names and asking about their families, just as I do with Kronites back home. In addition, I send greetings to regional Kronites celebrating holidays such as Diwali (the Indian festival of lights) and Chinese New Year. These small actions, practiced continuously, communicate respect for our employees, giving Kronites a sense of connection to the company.

"It's very important to us," Jaime says of my visits, "because we feel that our CEO cares about us, and how [our business] is working in Mexico. He wants to hear not only the good things, but also the challenges we have—how he can help us."

Our culture's commitment to family first also renders us more open and welcoming to people of other cultures. By prioritizing family so explicitly, we instantly create bonds and find common ground across cultural boundaries. "A message about family values works very well in China," says Max, our country manager there. "People understand that and very easily connect it back to Chinese culture." The pervasive sense of Kronos as a family itself also provides us with a conceptual framework for understanding and accommodating difference. James, in India, explains: "It's much easier to reconcile differences when you consider yourself as belonging to a single entity, the family. Within that family, each of us has our different personalities, attitudes, styles, and skills. But that overriding umbrella exists, and at Kronos it allows us to amalgamate a myriad of cultures."

In describing our culture as "global-ready," I don't mean to suggest that our organization is perfectly open-minded and global in its orientation. Dave, a Kronite who led efforts to enhance our international business through what we called our Global Growth Office, notes that issues like distance, language, and local work practices sometimes create misunderstandings and misplaced expectations. On one occasion, leaders wondered why we weren't selling more of our products in Germany. Although at first glance it might have seemed that our disappointing sales owed to a performance failure on the part of our sales team, it turned out that a cultural issue was at play. Germans have stringent expectations about the privacy of their data, and weren't comfortable with a cloud solution in which data would be hosted outside of their country. We expanded our approach and wound up offering German customers the option of hosting their data within Germany.

Geographic and cultural distance can also make it more difficult for Kronites around the world to get the attention of teams back home in the corporate office so that they can resolve problems as they arise. Several years ago, our Latin America operation ran into trouble when a Brazilian customer in the hospitality business asked for special adjustments to our products so that they would better fit its specific needs. It was hard for our Kronites in Latin America to obtain the support they needed from colleagues elsewhere in the company. Seeing how great this business opportunity was for us, senior leaders jumped in to help facilitate the desired product adjustments. Within 30 days, the adjustments were made, and our sales effort succeeded. That customer in Brazil now has 600 of its restaurants using our software. In retrospect, the episode represented a great learning opportunity as to what it takes to become a successful global enterprise. As we discovered, being global requires that employees concentrate extra hard on listening to the needs of their colleagues from different cultures and understanding their local requirements. This need for extra attention extends to small practices that inform our daily work. As Dave notes, "We used to have a lot of 3 a.m. meetings set up for folks in Asia, just because others in the organization forgot to consider time zone differences." We've made progress on that issue, but similar issues still crop up. "We've been international for a long time," Dave observes. "We're still learning how to be global."

Notwithstanding such difficulties, our culture has greatly facilitated our global expansion, allowing us to leverage the power of our people in distant markets. "Whenever I visit our international offices, I'm always amazed at how well our culture has traveled, especially the openness to learning and the sense of trust," Dave says. If tension still exists between the twin needs for standardization and adaptation to local markets, it helps a great deal that our corporate culture values inclusion, kindness, respect, and trust. Simply by applying that culture as evenly as possible, we can bring our people together while simultaneously respecting their uniqueness and granting them autonomy over their slices of the business.

OPTIMIZING YOUR CULTURE FOR GLOBAL GROWTH

Mindful of how challenging a global strategy can be even with a strong, unifying culture in place, we've taken a number of additional steps to encourage employees and our organization to better respect everyone's culture, regardless of where they work. We've even gone beyond cultural difference, strongly encouraging Kronites to respect one another regardless of their national origin, religion, gender, and race and other forms of diversity. If you run a global organization or team, consider the following:

Focus Team Members Explicitly on Global Issues and Perspectives

No matter how much respect your organization or you personally show for different cultures, cultural misalignments will still crop up, and people throughout the organization will at times fail to appreciate the unique circumstances and norms of local markets. A company also risks missing opportunities it never knew existed when employees and managers unduly focus on their own immediate contexts.

Recognizing that we had work to do in this area, we decided to make a global focus an explicit part of our WorkInspired culture. In Chapter 4, I described how we codified our culture by defining three core competencies—character, competence, and collaboration—and based 40 percent of Kronites' performance evaluation on how well they lived those principles. In defining collaboration, we specifically included a plank called Global Perspective. As we explained, Kronites who embrace a global perspective will keep abreast of important trends that impact the business or organization, understand how our organization operates within a global context, and help other Kronites to adopt global approaches. Further, Kronites should endeavor to understand the "unique challenges and constraints involved" in working globally, and the "unique business dynamics across cultures."

By integrating Global Perspective into our core competencies, we instantly made it part of every Kronite's job description, ensuring that we would hold one another accountable for thinking globally. Although it's a never-ending process, U.S.-based Kronites across the organization have become more conscious of differences across markets and have made efforts to adjust. As Dave observes, those 3 a.m. meetings for colleagues in Asia stopped once we articulated expectations that employees maintain a global mindset. More generally, "it wasn't until we really started codifying some of these elements that the folks at headquarters started taking notice of our international team members and made sure that their voices were included."

Expose Team Members to Global Contexts

Jessica, an operations analyst on our marketing team, helps our sales and marketing teams deploy technology to automate their processes. After just a year and a half on the job, she decided she wanted to push herself out of her comfort zone and experience what it's like to work in a different culture. So she applied to our Marketing Exchange Program. Applicants to the program travel to another region in which Kronos operates and spend up to two weeks working with local teams on a specific project applicants have proposed. Recognizing that our sales force in the United Kingdom would benefit from learning how to use our customer relationship management tool, Jessica proposed traveling to the United Kingdom to conduct trainings. She also wanted to inform her U.K. colleagues about how teams in the United States had been onboarding customers from around the world once they'd signed on to our products. That way, these colleagues could better prepare customers in European markets for the process.

Jessica's proposal was approved, and in 2017 she spent two weeks in the United Kingdom. It was a great experience for her. Not only did she transfer valuable knowledge to her British colleagues, helping them to work more efficiently and serve customers better, but she developed her own presentation skills, discovering how to communicate ideas in ways that different audiences could understand and appreciate. Further, she built her confidence and forged new connections with her colleagues abroad. "It was a mix of excitement and nerves in arriving there," she said, "but the warm welcome I received was definitely a great feeling." As Jessica related, she became familiar with the entire U.K. operation during her trip, and she continues to stay in touch with a number of employees there after her return home.

To build a global sensibility in your workforce as well as a general spirit of openness, there's no better way than to allow employees to embed directly with teams in other regions. It's one thing to be aware of and respect cultural differences, quite another to actually experience them firsthand. Alumni of our Marketing Exchange Program report that the experience makes them more comfortable collaborating with employees in their home office, too. They've experienced how open their colleagues in other countries are to collaboration, and how interesting and refreshing their viewpoints are, so they become more willing to cross departmental or functional boundaries.

Another employee, Nichole, spent a week in Mexico helping our team plan KronosLIVE, a customer conference held in the region. An event manager responsible for strategy, promotion, and execution of KronosWorks, our large annual customer conference with 3,000 attendees, Nichole was excited to spread the best practices she had learned to help build the regional event. As she reported, she "felt like I was part of the team, and everyone welcomed me with open arms." Since returning to the United States, she has noticed that "the fact that I have had [the experience in Mexico] has made me more comfortable collaborating with groups that I'm not normally engaging with." She feels more open and eager to engage with others, is even more excited about her work at Kronos, and is more loyal to the company. As both Jessica and Nichole learned, working in and experiencing different cultures is *fun*. It adds energy, zest, and interest to your life. It pushes you in new directions, even as it helps you build new skills that you can apply in your work. Give more employees the opportunity to work abroad, and they'll come away loving their job and the company they work for.

As a Leader or Manager, Go as Far as You Can

It's important to open yourself up to different cultural traditions, as doing so sets the tone for the rest of your organization and team. In China, it's commonplace for employees to share an honorary meal with the boss. When I travel there and to other regions, I make a point of partaking in cultural traditions. Although I'm not a big drinker, I make a toast at each table of our employees, since Max, our China country manager, feels that this is appropriate, and I want to show my respect.

I make a point to actively engage with local employees and make them feel part of Kronos. The truth is that I never need to go too far, just show a bit of extra effort to accommodate regional traditions. Our non-U.S. Kronites respect how I try to meet them where *they* are, and they sense that I don't approach them with a sense of cultural superiority. They feel closer to the company because of it.

Pursue Diversity and Inclusion Generally

It's more difficult to instill an ethic of openness and respect for other cultures if your company or team itself isn't diverse, and if your organization doesn't openly embrace inclusion. We explicitly affirm to our employees our dedication to inclusion, and our deeply held respect for all employees, no matter their ethnic background, gender, or other points of difference. As I said in my e-mail to Kronites after the 2016 presidential election: "I want to make it clear that we continue to be fully supportive of our employees of all backgrounds, faiths, and genders, no matter where they live, who they love, or where they worship." These aren't just words: they inform how managers and leaders at Kronos behave day-to-day. And as our engagement survey indicates, employees do feel welcomed. In July 2017, 79 percent of Kronites agreed with the statement, "Good ideas are adopted here regardless of who suggests them or where they come from"—significantly above the industry norm of 68 percent. In our industry, only 72 percent of employees agree with the statement that their company "encourages and promotes diversity of backgrounds, talents, and perspective." At Kronos, 90 percent of employees do.

Despite numbers like these, we know we still have work to do on diversity and inclusion, as does the technology industry generally. Our percentage of ethnically diverse employees runs above the industry average, but it's still lower than we'd like it to be. We've worked hard in this area over the years, but like other technology companies, we contend with a limited talent pool in many of our specific functions. As an industry leader, we have an opportunity to help deepen this pool over time. Doing that would benefit Kronos as well as the technology industry over all. Likewise, our small executive committee (my direct reports) as of this writing is not diverse. To a great extent, this is an unintended consequence of our success with our culture. We've had very little turnover among this group, even though recruiters regularly seek to lure these leaders away. As a result, the opportunities we've had to elevate new faces to the very top at Kronos have been limited over the past decade.

We have made great strides in improving diversity at levels of management just below the executive committee, outperforming our industry peers in this area. Consider gender. As of 2018, women composed 37 percent of our workforce, as opposed to only 30 percent overall in the technology sector. Of Kronites reporting directly to the executive suite, 47 percent are women. At every level of our organization, we have more women as a percentage of our employees than our industry peers do. The presence of these women gives us strength to draw on when executive level and other senior level positions open up. Over the past 12 months, more than 50 percent of all promotions to vice president have been women—all very well deserved. And I believe we'll see even more progress going forward thanks to our efforts in this area. Our Women in Business program seeks to address challenges facing women in business today and promotes career and personal development, offering Kronites a chance to partake in special events, mentorships, and networking. Among other programs, we also hold a well-attended Women's Leadership Forum every year to promote career and personal development and engage women to be active leaders within Kronos.

Our attempts to empower women reinforce the message that Kronos welcomes *everyone*. That spirit of inclusivity carries over when Kronites encounter colleagues from other cultures. Our organization is open to learning from colleagues throughout the world and adapting to their needs. We're all a part of the Kronos family.

Get Help When You Need It

When cultural misunderstandings or misalignments crop up— and they do—adapt quickly. But sometimes, your company might not understand where the misunderstanding originates, or what to do about it. In these cases, don't hesitate to bring in outside help.

When we started doing business in India and began hiring Kronites there, we found that weeks later when it came time for their first day of work, they didn't show up. Again and again this happened, and we weren't sure why. So we hired consultants who understood the local labor market, and the India culture generally. As we discovered, new hires in India didn't feel closely bound to the company before they started working here. It was customary to give 90 days' notice to their previous employers, and as we all know, a lot can happen in 90 days. Families were also exerting significant influence over young people's employment decisions, in some cases persuading our new hires to stay at their previous jobs or go elsewhere. We realized that we needed to be far more proactive in engaging with our new hires after they'd signed an offer letter, but before they showed up for their first days. That included keeping in touch with them, their spouses, their parents, and other important people in their lives, and even inviting them to tour our offices. We weren't just hiring a person, but a whole family! We rolled out what we called our "Red Carpet" program to help our new hires feel as if they were already a valued part of Kronos (which they were). Whereas we might have muddled through without a consultant and figuring out a new best practice on our own, owning up to what we didn't know and bringing in the needed help allowed us to adapt quickly and improve our operations.

KEEP GROWING CLOSER

I don't pretend we have the perfect recipe for running a global company, or that our culture is perfectly globalized. But I do think that focusing our organization on respecting other cultures, and on enabling employees in all of our offices to feel a strong attachment to our corporate headquarters, has taken us a long way. It helps explain why we have kept engagement levels above national averages everywhere we operate.

Today, we're pushing to remedy our deficiencies and become even more culturally sensitive. As one employee observed, "The company is very 'Boston' focused, so remote employees, or people in small offices, often seem excluded."[1] That's valid. Recognizing that our employee experience has traditionally been stronger at our corporate headquarters than at many of our other locations, we are moving to extend what we offer locally to Kronites who work elsewhere. In October 2017, we held a memorable event at our corporate headquarters not only to recognize the grand opening of our new headquarters but to celebrate our fortieth anniversary. I will forever remember the pride I felt as a marching band from a local university performed in our building's lobby, as the lieutenant governor of Massachusetts and other leaders gave speeches, and as we played a video greeting from our company's founder, my brother Mark.

On that same day, about 20 of our offices around the world gathered to watch a live stream of our corporate event via a social media channel. Like us at headquarters, they marked the occasion by decorating their workplaces and by passing out special treats to eat. In the future, we plan to extend other Kronos events to our global offices, helping to strengthen the sense of connection Kronites feel to our headquarters and to our corporate culture. At our most recent Take Your Child to Work Day event, 250 children participated in 13 locations around the world. When it comes to culture, distance shouldn't matter.

What more can you do to tie your faraway teammates closer together? If your organization or team celebrates traditional American holidays like Thanksgiving, can you also find ways of marking holidays that your non-U.S. workers hold dear? Can you communicate more frequently with your team members around the world? When you spend time with them, can you stretch a bit more and adopt their customs? Can you give your team members in different countries a bit more latitude than you otherwise might, signaling that you respect their judgment? Can you think of new ways to give members of your team direct exposure to your non-U.S. markets? Finally, can you better ensure that elements of your culture that build engagement with one part of your workforce apply equally to all employees?

Respecting everyone's culture requires extra effort, and at times, courage. But you don't have to be perfect to see extraordinary results. We've brought Kronites together, fostering high engagement around the world, even though we continue to learn and grow in this area. As Peter, the head of our Australian operations, says: "From the moment you join Kronos, you are part of the family. It doesn't matter which culture or country you are from." We might not always understand one another or attend to one another's needs, but when it comes to creating a global workplace that people love, a friendly smile, an outstretched hand, and a genuine willingness to listen go a long way.

Put Yourself Out
of Business

What do you do when your business is growing steadily, your financials are in great shape, your customers love your products and services, your employees are happy, and everything in general is running smoothly? Easy, some people say. Keep going. If it ain't broke, don't fix it.

At Kronos, we have a different answer.

In 2013, we were flying high as a company, approaching $1 billion in revenues on the strength of our successful Workforce Central‎ and Kronos Workforce Ready‎ software platforms, and entering entirely new markets. By almost any measure, we were performing well. Our transformation into a cloud company was proceeding smoothly. Our workforce was highly engaged. Our customers were happy. And yet, some of us were worried. We didn't think that our existing products would be enough to guarantee our future success.

We decided to take proactive measures. We created within our company a start-up of about 25 people, consisting of veteran Kronites with deep experience in workforce management, industry experts from outside the workforce management space, and recent college graduates with interesting backgrounds outside our industry. By including diverse perspectives, we planned to spark fruitful discussions and generate new insights about our industry and our offerings. We gave this team a $5 million budget, an office about 20 miles away from our corporate headquarters, and a yearlong assignment: put Kronos out of business. This team was to focus without distraction on creating a product that was far superior to anything we offered at that time. They were to work in a stripped-down start-up environment—using mobile devices instead of wired phones, collaborative workspaces instead of private offices. Unlike a real disruptive start-up that might one day challenge us, this team would have full access to all Kronos resources, and they'd understand our strengths and weaknesses in great detail. Go crazy, we told them. Irritate one another!

Every six weeks or so, I met with Kronites from our "start-up" to learn about its latest discoveries. On my first visit, I wasn't terribly impressed by what I heard. *Gosh,* I thought during my drive home, *are these ideas really our future?* But over time, the team's thinking evolved, and I drove home from my periodic visits increasingly excited.

About nine months into it, the team formally presented a proposal for an innovative product, code-named "Falcon." Our leadership team reviewed the proposal and came away as impressed as I was. Although it was risky, we decided to develop Falcon, bring it to market, and if we succeeded, put Kronos in its present incarnation out of business. We then assigned 600 employees to Falcon and invested $150 million, a sizable sum for us.

In 2017, we launched Falcon and officially named the new product Workforce Dimensions, a completely new cloud platform that reimagined every part of our previous one—the underlying technology, user experience, functionality, integration, data access, delivery, and support. This platform was cutting-edge in our industry—faster, easier, more accessible, more connected, and smarter than anything out there. It was also embedded with cutting-edge technologies like artificial intelligence, machine learning, and embedded analytics. If ever there was a product that could put our existing platform out of business, this was it! As one analyst raved, Workforce Dimensions was "a complete rethink of how Kronos delivers workforce management capability. It's not just a new skin, or the old product scaled to fit a phone screen."[1] Another called our development process "truly remarkable."[2]

Our willingness to invest heavily in this project reflects the pivotal importance of innovation in our culture. Since our founding, we've continuously innovated our products, adding new features, algorithms, and design elements. On five separate occasions, we've taken big leaps, embracing new technologies and fundamentally reinventing ourselves as a company. When we launched Kronos, our product was a time clock with a microprocessor inside. Then we launched Timekeeper Central®, our first PC-based product. Then we introduced Workforce Central, our first client-server product, followed by our first web-based product. Most recently, we transitioned from selling licensed software to adopt a cloud, SaaS business model.

If we've long regarded innovation as part of our product strategy, embedding it in our tagline, Workforce Innovation That Works, we've also come to see innovation as a key part of our *people* strategy. If you want to engage your workforce, you can't just nurture them, trust them, communicate with them, show respect for them, and manage them in the ways I've discussed. You also have to give them the opportunity to put their *own* stamp on the business. You have to give them permission to take risks and innovate. Further, you have to make innovation part of the culture, extending it to *every* part of your business, not just technology and products. In addition to investing more than $500 million over the past five years on product innovation, we've adopted an array of programs over the past decade designed to empower Kronites to take risks and think creativity. Our executives have led the charge, modeling innovation in their behavior and encouraging it in their teams. The result has been a culture that not merely accepts positive change, but actively and aggressively pursues it.

Many executives talk about putting themselves out of business, but their companies often fail to deliver. At Kronos, we remake our existing businesses all the time, in ways big and small. Our people notice this, and they tell us how much it impacts their job satisfaction. As one of our boomerang employees remarked, "I value the way we are constantly collaborating to innovate and not only stay relevant, but lead with new innovations." Another told us that Kronos, "makes me feel entrepreneurial. The mission is clear and through my efforts, I can make a difference to the success of the team and our customers. I am supported to be creative and accountable."

Whether you're leading or managing within a larger, established company or a start-up, don't just talk about innovation. Dedicate yourself and your teams to rethinking and improving how you operate. Galvanize people to take risks and present new ideas. Invest in those ideas, and execute on them. Be bold. Take risks. Experiment. Put yourself out of business!

DRIVING INNOVATION AT THE ORGANIZATIONAL LEVEL

In our age of disruption, most companies are already trying hard to innovate, if not to engage their workforce, then to provide the greatest possible value to customers. The question for many companies is thus how to intensify and magnify existing efforts like never before, so that a spirit of innovation defines the culture, inspiring all employees to come up with new ideas. I don't claim we have the secret that will turn any company into an innovation powerhouse. I can, however, share some policies, programs, and principles that have worked for us.

As we've seen, one of the first steps to take when trying to infuse the entire culture with any specific quality or value is to define it formally for employees. In unveiling our core competencies, we specifically mentioned innovation under our "competence" plank, defining it as follows: "Generates and champions new ideas, approaches, and initiatives, and creates an environment that nurtures and supports innovation. Leverages fresh perspectives, breakthrough ideas, and new paradigms to create value in the market. Encourages new ways of looking at problems, processes, or solutions." What does innovation mean to your business? Should responsibility for innovation fall on certain people or teams in particular, or on everyone? Are there specific forms of innovation you wish to encourage? Does innovation tend to happen primarily on an individual basis, or is collaboration on novel ideas or approaches more important?

Defining innovation will have little impact if you don't also invest in programs and policies that encourage all employees to innovate. Our functional groups offer an array of developmental programs for Kronites. In our products and technology group, for instance, employees until recently participated in "Kronovation

Days" several times a year. At these designated times, they worked on projects that normally fall beyond the scope of their daily jobs. They had the time and freedom to explore new ideas and push their own boundaries. At the end of the Kronovation event, employees presented their ideas to their peers, and managers offered awards for the most promising ideas, some of which we incorporated into our products as features. We've taken a hiatus from Kronovation Days since kicking off Workforce Dimensions. So much innovation was occurring around Workforce Dimensions that our leaders in engineering judged it unnecessary to devote more time specifically to innovation. But Kronovation Days were a popular program, so if we ever need them again, they'll be back!

Another step to take to instill innovation in your culture is to support employee communication and collaboration. Although it took some adjustment on the part of Kronites, our internal collaboration platform has become a vibrant place for employees around the world to connect with one another and share new ideas. Like other companies, we've also developed innovative physical workspaces. Our new corporate headquarters has an entire floor outfitted with an array of spaces designed for collaboration. Kronites can huddle together in our coffee/smoothie bar, hash out problems together over games of foosball or Ping-Pong, or stroll together through our indoor park (see Chapter 6). Other floors offer a range of additional meeting areas, all equipped with state-of-the-art technology to project images from laptops. Kudos to our IT department. In recent years, we've also redesigned many other Kronos offices around the world to maximize opportunities for innovation.

If your team or organization is serious about fostering innovation, you also have to measure it. We evaluate managers based on their ability to foster innovation and responsible risk-taking. In our Manager Effectiveness Index (MEI) and engagement assessments (Chapter 4), we ask employees to indicate their agreement with various statements that touch on innovation, such as, "My manager encourages our work group to take appropriate risks to improve business results." We also include questions measuring the extent to which employees feel we are generally offering a culture of collaborative problem solving that leads to innovative solutions. We ask Kronites to tell us whether they agree that: "conditions at Kronos make it safe to challenge the status quo," "the people in my work group adapt easily to new ways of doing things," and "at Kronos, we anticipate changes taking place in the business environment before they happen."

LEADING INNOVATION

Aside from implementing organizational policies and programs that encourage a culture of innovation, leaders and managers should also adopt a number of key behaviors:

Listen to and Implement Employee Ideas

In 2012, Tim, one of our Australian employees, came up with an idea for changing how we implement our software. Previously, a Kronite would often have to visit a customer and manually install our software on servers. Tim thought this process was too lengthy—days or potentially weeks of wasted time—so he took it upon himself to write a software program that performed automated software installations. He showed the program to his boss and others, and with their encouragement, proceeded to add in features that allowed customers to configure and test this software as they needed. Then he and his colleagues took his program a step further, adding in features that compiled all the industry and company data we were already collecting from customers in order to configure their products. Further, Tim and his colleagues had the program identify common patterns and then use those patterns to recommend standard configurations for customers in specific industries. With these standard configurations as a starting point, 80 percent of the implementation task was already done. All we had to do with new customers was continue to configure the product so that it conformed to the specific nuances of their businesses and industries.

Overall, this implementation methodology, which we named Kronos Paragon™ cut customer implementation costs by millions of dollars, allowing us to dramatically reduce the time it took for customers to begin extracting value from our products. Kronites everywhere can look to Paragon as proof that innovation isn't just talk at our company—it's real. As Tim notes, leaders and managers always did a good job of encouraging him to develop Paragon: "They gave us freedom to explore ideas that they thought would have merit."

Give Employees the Space to Develop Ideas on Their Own

Tim further points to the autonomy his managers allowed him and his colleagues when it came to developing Paragon: "They'd say, 'That's a good idea. Let's regroup in a month to see how it's looking. If it looks good, we'll pursue.'" I gave my team similar autonomy when we tried to put ourselves out of business with Workforce Dimensions, checking in every six weeks, but otherwise trusting the leaders I'd appointed to deliver. I'm not claiming organizations can't establish deep cultures of innovation when the CEO is deeply involved. At Apple, Steve Jobs delved into all aspects of new product design, a practice that hardly prevented his company from developing a legendary capacity to innovate. But leaders can take different approaches to fostering innovation and still succeed. As I've found at Kronos, a supportive, trusting, and hands-off approach has empowered people to deliver incredibly innovative solutions to push our business forward.

When I say hands-off, I don't mean leaders and managers shouldn't exercise strong oversight. They should. With all the latitude I gave our Workforce Dimensions team, I didn't hesitate to make key decisions that influenced their process. When the team originally came to me and said they wanted five years to bring a new product to market, I said no—they had one year. We wound up negotiating two years. Of course, I also agreed to providing the resources they needed so that they could meet that deadline. Later, I pushed the deadline back, giving the team more time to add functionality that our customers expected. Having researched other companies, I insisted that we achieve "feature parity" with our existing products—our new product had to do everything that our existing one already did. Toward the end of our development process, I pushed the deadline back once again so that the team could incorporate suggestions that we'd solicited from several of our larger customers. I made these key decisions, but I didn't interfere with the substance of the process itself. Our team knew the details of the project much better than I did. Why wouldn't I defer to them on most decisions?

Model the Reasonable Risk-Taking You Wish to See in Your People

It's harder to convince employees to take chances on good ideas if you're not doing so yourself. The riskiest decision I've made as CEO has been taking our company private. When I first floated that possibility, our board and other leaders were firmly against it. "It'll be a disaster," they told me, "you'll have 25-year-old MBAs at some private-equity firm running the company." Yet I learned through extensive research and thinking that going private really was in the best interest of our company and our shareholders, so I stuck with it. I'm glad I did! It took us 30 years to reach $600 million in revenues. Since we went private, it took us just 11 years to grow to $1.4 billion. We no longer had to think quarter to quarter, and instead could adopt strategies that were in our long-term interest, but that might have required some up-front investments and sacrifices. We could be nimble and change directions quickly if we found that a specific course of action wasn't working for us. We could also act more confidently, rather than feeling like analysts and investors were second-guessing us every quarter. On other occasions, our attempts to take the business in new directions have faltered. But I continue to experiment, and I encourage others around me to do the same. You might take a hit at times, but think of what you'll gain over the long term if you get in the habit of seeking out and pursuing potentially great ideas. And if nothing else, you'll inspire everyone around you to take risks, too.

Encourage Innovation in Every Part of Your Business

Some leaders and managers who support innovation unwittingly limit the sphere in which they apply new thinking. That's a mistake. To really get your workforce's creative juices churning, demonstrate how open you are to changing your policies and processes, not just for technology and new products. Over the past several years, as we've pursued product innovation via Workforce Dimensions, our executive team has also innovated our human resource policies, implementing myTime and making many other important changes. We've also innovated our marketing, unveiling our first radio campaigns after years of focus on print advertising, and investing in our sales and customer events to make them much more sophisticated, inspiring, and entertaining.

These instances are really just the beginning. On a broader scale, we've innovated our business model, becoming a cloud SaaS company, a shift that has required transformation throughout our company. Guided by a team of consultants we hired, we've redesigned entire functions, rebuilt our IT infrastructure, created a new customer success organization, streamlined and simplified our sales processes, and mobilized new communication tools to make our organization much more customer-centric, collaborative, and accountable. We created a special Transformation Management Office (TMO) to help us organize and execute all of this change.

Rapid innovation across our company hasn't always been easy for Kronites. When we first decided to move to the cloud, many employees and managers were upset. As Chris, one of our senior leaders, remembers, "People didn't like it. They were grumpy. We fought with one another, and everyone's babies were called ugly."[3] Within a year, however, Kronites became less fearful and even excited about the changes. They saw customers showing interest, and they also were reassured by new incentive plans that we put in place to ensure that our new business model benefited them as well. The spirit of innovation became even more deeply embedded in our culture.

By 2018, more than 11 million people were using Kronos cloud offerings, up from virtually zero in 2012, and virtually all of our net new customers were selecting a cloud solution. Kronites feel proud of that success, and they understand that in the eyes of their leaders, virtually everything and anything about our business is susceptible to improvement. They are even more inspired to inject new thinking into their work. Their engagement rises in turn.

LET YOUR PEOPLE FLY

In recent years, when I've told people that Kronos was working on a new product that would put its existing flagship Workforce Central product out of business, they've reacted skeptically. "You'll destroy your existing business. You'll go backward. You can't do two things at the same time. Nobody has ever pulled that off." I've always listened politely, nodding my head, but saying to myself, "Yeah, but those other companies aren't us, and we're not them."

I always believed we could make it work—not because I thought our underlying vision for the product and our industry's future was correct, which I did, but because I believed in our people and our culture. After 40 years of product innovation, and a decade in which we'd not only implemented programs to boost innovation but transformed the entire company, I felt that we could innovate and improve just about anything if we put our minds to it, even our flagship product. Could we have succeeded with a project as ambitious as Workforce Dimensions if innovation at Kronos had been merely lackluster? Maybe not. And that leads me to a final thought on innovation: if you're interested in creating a workplace that employees love, take steps to unleash their creative talents, but start at a place that's realistic and not overly disruptive. Work with the culture you have, and move steadily toward the culture to which you aspire. Experiment with some of the programs and policies I've described, and throw in some others that you come up with. Above all, have fun! Before long, your employees will enjoy their jobs more, too, and will feel even more excited to come to work. As an added benefit, you'll position your company to become a leader in its industry, not merely a follower.

I can't end this chapter without recounting a memorable episode from our Workforce Dimensions project. I absolutely *swear* it happened. Nine months into the project, after the team had proposed its ideas and a plan of action to our leadership team, we reached the point where the company needed to decide whether to invest fully in the project. One afternoon, members of our Workforce Dimensions leadership team and I sat together in the only conference room at the Workforce Dimensions team's rented offices. The space was located on the first floor of a building, its floor-to-ceiling windows giving us a view of a large tree.

"So," we said to one another, "are we really going to do this? Is it worth the risk?" As we were talking it through one last time, a large bird of prey flew down and landed on a branch of this tree. Was it a falcon? I'm no expert on birds, so I couldn't tell you. But it was big and confident, and it was looking right at us, as if to say, "Come on, say yes! You know, I've been circling this building for nine months, it's time!" We all looked on, stunned.

The bird sat there for a moment or two. Then it flapped its wings and flew off. "Done!" we said. "Let's fund it."

True story. And the moral is simple: innovation is nothing if not a great adventure, for you, your company, and most of all, your people. So, go for it. Let your people fly.

Empower the
Next Generation

Eleven-year-old Ravi and his 10-year-old sister, Shalinee, live with their three siblings in the small village of Mamura in India. With their father working odd jobs for a daily wage and their mother disabled, their family barely covers its basic needs. To supplement the family's meager earnings, Ravi became a rag-picker, delving into piles of trash and searching for objects to sell. Attending school was far too expensive, so Shalinee spent her days at home, looking after her younger siblings.

That is, until Kronos stepped in. In 2015, we opened the Kronos Noida Learning Center in nearby Noida, India, not far from one of our facilities in India. The learning center's mission: support the education and healthy development of under-privileged children in the local area. Ravi and Shalinee began coming to the center in 2016, receiving free uniforms, instruction in academic subjects, life-skills training, personal counseling, and healthy snacks to supplement their diets. Over a period of months, the siblings made significant academic progress and improved their communication skills. Instead of rag-picking, they are doing what kids everywhere should do—attending school and preparing for the future.

The Kronos Noida Learning Center is one of many projects we fund as part of our GiveInspired corporate social responsibility program. We organize our giving around a specific cause that we've found especially relevant when it comes to engagement: empowering the next-generation workforce. Our primary focus is to encourage the advancement of science, technology, engineering, and math (STEM) skills required of tomorrow's workforce. We've done that by supporting an array of career and educational programs for youth.

I've long believed that businesses have a moral responsibility to help train the next generation of employees. But empowering the next generation also helps mobilize the current workforce. What is more inspiring for employees than knowing they've had a hand in helping a young person to thrive? Instead of merely donating money, we take an active role, supporting youth by bringing them into Kronos in a number of capacities. Employees love it, as they gain exposure to new ideas and feel more energy and dynamism among their teams.

In Chapter 6, I talked about how important it is to inject fun into your culture. Who loves working in a place that isn't fun? A similar point holds true for youthfulness. Who wants to work in a place that seems old, stuck in its ways, aloof, unchanging? By nurturing the next generation workforce, we make our culture feel spirited and dynamic, complementing the impact of other cultural elements like our cutting-edge workplaces and our strong emphasis on innovation. Nurturing youth also allows us to give back to society, making Kronites proud. Engagement soars, taking our business with it.

ENGAGING EMPLOYEES THROUGH CORPORATE GIVING

Our emphasis on empowering the next generation has been a relatively recent development. For most of our company's history, we allocated funds to an array of local and national charities. We tended to spread ourselves too thin, making small, haphazard donations in response to requests from nonprofits that approached us. As a result, we supported a miscellany of groups and causes, including golf tournaments and local associations and events. We also didn't stay in touch with the charities to which we donated, so we weren't certain of the impact our dollars were having.

At around the time we were codifying our core competencies, a group of us sat in a budget meeting and posed several long-overdue questions: Why was our corporate giving so piecemeal and disorganized? Why weren't we pursuing philanthropy in ways that align with our company's core purpose (helping organizations effectively manage their workforces)? Our queries prompted a spirited dialogue, which in turn led to a coherent vision for our corporate giving program: "To support the next-generation workforce in the communities where we work and live."

We gave our newly formalized corporate giving program a name—GiveInspired, a sub-brand of WorkInspired—to align it formally with our culture. From there, we developed criteria for vetting the many requests for philanthropic gifts that we received. First and foremost, we'd give to local, national, and international organizations that helped youth prepare for future jobs and careers. Second, we'd give to local organizations that served communities where we operate, mainly but not exclusively in the arena of education and youth. Third, in keeping with our ethic of caring for people, we also decided to support organizations that helped communities respond to disasters. And fourth, we would fund additional initiatives that somehow helped our customers or the Kronos brand. To administer our annual budget, we formed an internal corporate giving committee, which drew from a cross-section of employees and managers. It wouldn't be me or other senior leaders who'd dictate our giving—it would be Kronites themselves.

In the years that our GiveInspired corporate giving committee has existed, we've donated to an array of programs around the world that support youth and their careers. In the local area surrounding our corporate headquarters, for instance, we now support summer programs for 2,500 youth through the United Way, as well as programs through the local chapter of the Boys & Girls Clubs. To enhance the impact of our charitable giving, we've also begun making active, unsolicited grants, a practice that allows us to forge long-term partnerships and measure the impact of our giving more closely. As an example, we've worked with the University of Massachusetts at Lowell (UMass Lowell), whose campus is located near our corporate headquarters, to create a suite of programming. Our Kronos Scholars Co-Op program now brings students at the university to Kronos for a six-month learning experience each year. At the end of the program, we give each student a scholarship, and we offer the best and brightest among them permanent jobs at Kronos if we have relevant openings. To date, over 70 students have gone through the program, and many have been hired as Kronites.

Another organization we've helped on an ongoing basis through grant-making is United Teen Equality Center (UTEC), a group that engages at-risk youth and helps them to "trade violence and poverty for social and economic success."[1] To date, UTEC's unique approach has had an astonishing record of success, combining aggressive outreach to at-risk youth with mentoring, skills training, and work opportunities. In the state of Massachusetts, over half of young adults who have been incarcerated are rearrested within a year. But of the young people who enrolled in UTEC in 2017, 89 percent stayed out of trouble, and almost all (99 percent) had no new criminal convictions on their records. A full 83 percent of the organization's graduates are currently employed. By helping to support UTEC, Kronos empowers students and elevates the quality of life in our local community.

Offering financial support is only one part of philanthropy at Kronos. We don't just want our employees to witness the organization empowering the next-generation workforce. We want them to have the opportunity to volunteer their time, so that the spirit of helping youth and of giving becomes part of the fabric of our culture. We strongly encourage Kronites to take on charitable projects individually and with their teams, including those unrelated to the next-generation workforce. In addition, we formally encourage Kronites to leverage our open time off policy to volunteer for causes they find meaningful. Although Kronites and their teams can select any cause, many of them do choose those that help empower the next generation workforce. At our Noida, India, office, Kronites volunteer regularly at the school we support there. As Ashok, head of our Noida operation, relates, employees "are like buddies to these children at the center and go on weekends. . . . This close relationship has helped the children get a larger purview of the world and has inspired them to work hard in redefining their future."

As you might expect, participation with this project and related ones has also helped Kronites feel more connected to our company. As part of our annual employee engagement survey, we ask employees to rate their happiness with our corporate social responsibility initiatives. Over a three-year period, that score has swung dramatically upward in our Noida location, moving from 73 percent (i.e., 73 percent of Kronites in Noida gave our corporate social responsibility programs one of the top two possible ratings) to 96 percent. As Kronites tell us, volunteering with the children is a deeply meaningful, almost spiritual experience for them. "Everyone wishes to relive their childhood," one Noida-based Kronite relates. "[The Kronos Noida Learning Center] gives me a chance to do so. Every time you visit, you are refueled with so much happiness, optimism, and fun. I volunteer because it continuously teaches me something new about people, about cooperation, compassion, and about myself." Another Kronite says: "Spending time with the children is an integral part of my Kronos experience."

Kronites elsewhere have had similar experiences—and feel more excited about Kronos and their jobs—thanks to the time they spend volunteering. In Sydney, Australia, Kronites brought Christmas gifts to at-risk women, partnering with an organization that aims to empower and enable these women to make real changes in their lives. "Such a humbling experience," one Kronite wrote on our internal collaboration platform. Another wrote: "A very rewarding experience indeed. What a way to spend a day! I am very thankful to Kronos for providing such an opportunity." One Kronite used myTime to participate in a bike charity ride benefiting the Arava Institute for Environmental Studies, an educational organization in the Middle East that brings youth together from different cultures around environmental issues. As this Kronite wrote, he originally was somewhat skeptical about the institute and its work. Could it really help these youth bridge their differences? "But when I saw all those students from Israel, Jordan, and Palestine, and other countries studying, working, and living together, trying to build up the trust between [such] different cultures, my skepticism was broken. My experience . . . was eye and heart opening, and I see it now as a beacon of hope in the Middle East."

Experiences helping the younger generation are so powerful that they often stay with Kronites for years afterward. One of our senior leaders, Barb, recalls how about a decade ago our sales group assembled bicycles in small groups as a team-building exercise. What team members didn't realize was that at the conclusion of the event, about 100 children would arrive in person to claim these bikes as donations. "People were moved to tears," Barb says. In her view, experiences like this have made a "huge" impression on her team members. Even today, she says, employees and managers still talk about the bicycle-assembly event, as well as numerous other volunteer experiences they've had at Kronos.

INTERNS, INTERNS EVERYWHERE

Beyond our charitable efforts, we've supported the next-generation workforce—and helped engage our own—by actively training young people ourselves. In addition to our Kronos Scholars Co-Op program, our annual summer internship program allows college students from around the globe to further their interest in STEM and the world of business by working a stint at Kronos.

We give interns real assignments to work on, not the typical busywork. Consider the experience of Meaghan, an intern with visual impairments. For years, we've worked on making our software more accessible for the visually impaired, but we weren't sure how much progress we were really making. To test our web and mobile applications, we recruited Meaghan to carefully assess our software and provide thoughtful feedback. Thanks to her input, we've made significant changes in our product, such as making it possible for blind employees to review and approve their timecard on a mobile device using a screen reader that vocalizes the user interface, or allowing people with other visual impairments to see their schedule in high contrast without relying on color codes. By engaging directly with our software developers, Meaghan helped infuse an awareness and empathy into our products, not only improving the user experience for people with disabilities, but usability in general.

Preparing the next-generation workforce means helping them build real skills and understand how meaningful and important work can—and should—be. And if our interns do real work, and if, like Meaghan, they make real contributions to Kronos, they should also receive above-market wages. We pay interns more in part because we want to attract the best and the brightest, in hopes that we might recruit some of them to become new Kronites (we wind up hiring about 15 to 20 percent of them).

Our internship program represents a significant investment on our part, but it's worth it—to the students and to us. Each year, we receive thousands of applications for about 100 spots. Interns post positive reviews of the program and our culture on job websites. As one wrote, "Internships here are absolutely amazing! We do real impactful work rather than administration and irrelevant, time-consuming tasks. We get to feel like what we bring to the table in regard to ideas, opinions, personality, etc. is valued and desired."

As for our employees, they get a chance to impact the lives of students. Some who wish to advance into management roles get to "try on" being a manager by overseeing interns during the summer. One employee in our marketing department who had expressed interest in being a manager developed valuable skills managing interns during the summer. From there, we advanced her into our JumpStart training program for new managers. Nine months later, this employee had hired and was overseeing two full-time team members. Our internship program wasn't pivotal in this Kronite's advancement—that would have happened without it. But having these initial management experiences definitely helped.

MORE WAYS TO SUPPORT ENGAGEMENT AND EMPOWER THE NEXT GENERATION

Hopefully, my discussion so far has not only highlighted how empowering the next generation can support employee engagement, but also sparked some ideas as to how you might pursue this principle in your own team or organization. Here are some additional best practices:

Make It a "Real" Priority

One reason companies sometimes fail to engage employees around their charitable or social responsibility initiatives is that they send mixed messages. They tout the company's commitment to particular social causes and encourage employees to get involved, but then they suggest—either implicitly or explicitly—that the company's "real" priorities should take precedence. We've succeeded with GiveInspired because we make clear that empowering the next generation—and giving back to the community generally—is in fact a real priority for our company. Our leadership team gives charitable efforts visibility in meetings alongside our other strategic goals, and we participate in them ourselves, both inside and outside of work. With Kronites enthusiastically sharing their experiences with youth on our internal collaboration platform, with managers throughout the company encouraging and organizing charitable activity for their teams, and with young people a visible presence throughout our organization, empowering the next generation becomes far more than an organizational priority. It becomes an inextricable and endearing part of the culture.

Embed Charitable Efforts into the Work Itself

Why distinguish so firmly between your "real" work and nurturing the next generation? Throughout Kronos, managers look for opportunities to connect our business and charitable activities. Doing so further communicates how seriously we take our charitable mission, and it provides hugely meaningful experiences for employees and customers within the context of the workday. Instead of taking a team bowling to celebrate a win or to bring team members closer together, our managers sometimes take them out for a day to beautify a school's grounds or deliver holiday gifts to needy children. Kronites love it. As one wrote after one such outing: "Personally, I've not been given this opportunity with [a] past employer and I felt it [was] an invaluable experience. I would recommend it to anyone. Not only does it bring you closer as a team but it gives you the opportunity to give back to your community."

Mobilize the Other WorkInspired Principles

You can use the principles in this book individually to enhance engagement, but they gain power when you deploy many of them together. Conceptually, GiveInspired embodies our emphasis on caring for others. But our execution of this initiative brings together many principles we've covered. I've mentioned how we've encouraged Kronites to use myTime to volunteer for charitable causes. By supporting local charitable efforts in the communities where we operate, we also reinforce the principle of welcoming our global employees—letting them choose and participate in charitable efforts that matter to *them*. Likewise, by using our internship program as an opportunity for young Kronites to gain management experience, we help support the principle of giving all employees a great manager. In imagining how your team or organization might support youth, think back through the principles we've covered in this book. How might you incorporate them here?

Stay Disciplined

Once you create a structured program for empowering the next generation, it's easy to slide back into a less disciplined approach, saying yes to charitable requests that seem worthy but don't fit your mission. Stay focused. In 2015, a personal acquaintance of mine asked Kronos to support a national program of his that helped foster businesses started by entrepreneurs in underprivileged communities. It was a great cause, and it supported our mission of empowering the next generation workforce. Still, at the time the request came in, this program wasn't operating in any of the local communities where we operated, so we declined to participate. A year later, my friend called again: the program was interested in expanding into Massachusetts's Merrimack Valley, where our headquarters is located. Perfect! Since we had done our research and knew that this program was high quality, we committed to fund training for these entrepreneurs so that they could then pitch investors at a national convention.

Stay Engaged—for the Right Reasons

Many companies tout the vast sums of money they donate to charitable causes. It might make for good public relations, but simply pulling out a checkbook won't get you far in terms of engagement. Ultimately, the success of GiveInspired has owed to the energy, time, and thought we've put into it. Employees need to see that the organization stands behind engaging the next generation workforce—that it's connected to everything else the organization does, and that the programs you support are high quality and deliver real value. If they do, your efforts will translate most effectively into greater affection for the company. We don't win awards for our charitable efforts because we write bigger checks, but because we make sure that every dollar we do spend makes the maximum difference, both for communities and for us.

MAKING A DIFFERENCE

One reason that empowering the next generation workforce resonates so strongly with us is that we see the incredible difference it makes in the lives of the younger generation that we help. We also see some of our own colleagues thriving in the workplace thanks to the helping hand they received at critical points in their lives. Kristina, one of our senior leaders, grew up in Hungary and emigrated to the United States via Austria and Canada. Through sheer determination and grit, she distinguished herself in her profession. But as she often points out, she didn't do it alone. "I've been so lucky and blessed to meet amazing individuals along the way," she says. "It's not that they give you free money or a free lunch. They're there for you, guiding you, coaching you, giving you advice and confidence along the way."

Stories like these epitomize all that can happen when we take responsibility for empowering the next generation. And now, through our programs at Kronos, this senior leader and other Kronites can provide similar support to other young people. They can contribute to a culture that prioritizes giving back, and that connects charitable giving profoundly and consistently with the work we do for our customers. In a culture like that, how could you *not* love your job? How could you not show up every day determined to help your company and its customers succeed?

EPILOGUE

In February 2018, after Kronos (for the first time!) was honored as one of the Fortune 100 Best Companies to Work For by the consulting firm Great Place to Work and *Fortune* magazine, an employee posted a note about the award on one of his personal social media channels. As he recounted, he had joined Kronos two years earlier, leaving a company that he felt "extremely passionate about, with products I believed in." Since then, when acquaintances have asked about his decision to leave his former employer to come to Kronos, he's replied, "I couldn't be more proud or happy to work . . . at an amazing company with an outstanding culture that allows us all to WorkInspired." Responding to this post, another Kronite added: "I feel the same way. After working for [several other] corporations, you quickly realize what a special place Kronos is. I am proud to work for Kronos!"

Think of it: an employee feels so excited about his company and his work that he takes it upon himself to communicate his feelings to his network on social media, reinforcing our culture and values, enhancing our reputation as an employer, and helping in our recruitment efforts. Another employee feels so passionately that she publicly endorses his message. Both employees compare our company favorably with other top companies for which they've worked. How remarkable! And how humbling.

When I started at Kronos as a 21-year-old, I never imagined I would be here four decades later as CEO, much less that we'd build a culture that would impact employees and their families so powerfully. I've written this book because we've created something special at Kronos, and I want to share it with the world.

I'm convinced that organizations in any industry can follow our lead and create high-performance environments in which people love to work. The principles and practices I've presented here haven't been easy to implement, but with concerted effort, we've made so much progress! We don't just talk about treating employees well. We actually deliver on it. Not perfectly. Not all the time. But as well as we can, and with an eye toward doing even better. We're committed to treating people as human beings, addressing a broad set of financial and emotional needs, so that employees feel both empowered and inspired to do their best. And when they do their best, when they're fully engaged, magic happens.

You don't have to implement every best practice I've described to improve engagement in your team or organization. Start with a few and go from there. Draw inspiration from our techniques and modify them to fit your existing culture. And apply the same approach to your own behavior. When you've mastered a few of the behaviors I describe, try a few more. Work on practicing them every day. Your employees might not respond right away, but stick with it. As motivational speaker and author Simon Sinek has observed, "There is no event, no [one] thing that I can tell you [to do that will make] your people trust you. It just doesn't work that way. It's an accumulation of lots and lots of little things."[1] I wholeheartedly agree, and it doesn't just apply to building trust, but to engagement generally. It takes many small, seemingly insignificant actions, performed consistently in the course of daily work, to foster the principles—humility, caring, open-mindedness, concern for the next generation—described in this book.

Staying focused on "people strategy" is the work of a lifetime. And as leaders of people, we have so much to gain. I can't tell you how joyful I feel when I hear what working at Kronos has meant to our employees. Over the years, my satisfaction as a leader has had little to do with the revenue our company has generated or the accolades we've received. It has had *everything* to do with the impact we've had on people. I've watched careers blossom. I've watched employees raise families and achieve their dreams. I've watched employees happily retire after enjoying long, satisfying careers. I've watched customers and partners achieve new levels of success because of the care and attention given to them by our inspired workforce. All of this is immensely gratifying—far more than fame or fortune ever could be. When you create a culture in which everyone loves to work, you set in motion a positive dynamic of inspiration that is all-encompassing, that produces remarkable business performance, that improves the lives of your people, and that draws you in, too.

Ultimately, the impact of engagement is enormous, much bigger than we often imagine. And so is our personal impact on those whom we manage and lead. What if employees and former employees were going out of their way to rave about your culture? What if they loved your company so much that they couldn't imagine ever working anywhere else? What if they consistently pushed your company's performance to new heights? And what if they inspired *you* so much that you wanted to stay at your company for the next 40 years? Take care of your people, support them, inspire them—and they will.

ACKNOWLEDGMENTS

"Who would want to read a book by *me?*" That's what I
blurted out when someone gently suggested I should
write a book. I followed with: "I'm not sure *I* would read a book
by me." After careful prodding, I came to recognize that perhaps
I did have ideas to share that others would find useful. And now,
some two years later, the remarkable journey of writing a book
has come to an end.

Michele Glorie, our head of corporate communications,
was by my side at every turn—this book would not have happened without her smart guidance and hard work. Partnering
with Seth Schulman, my contributing editor, has also been a joy.
Seth listened to my story, asked probing questions, and helped
me choose the right words to convey my reflections on almost 40
years of work at Kronos. I send a heartfelt thank you to my agent,
Jim Levine, for his interest and insight, and also for leading me to
Casey Ebro at McGraw-Hill, whose keen editorial eye has made
this a much better book.

So many leaders, managers, and employees at Kronos have
contributed to this book, whether by agreeing to sit for interviews,
responding to requests for information, or reviewing parts or all
of the book at various stages. Thank you so much for your generosity of time and spirit—I truly appreciate it. I also wish to thank
the Kronos leadership team past and present, as well as our current and past board members for the support they've provided
me over the years. A special thank you goes out to my longtime
assistant at Kronos, Joanne Johansen. It would be impossible to

describe all that Joanne has done for me and my family—she is simply the kindest, most thoughtful, most caring person I know!

My career at Kronos wouldn't have been possible without my wife of 35 years. Susan, you are a perfect partner! Thank you for your endless support and encouragement. My daughters, Danielle and Hillary, have taught me priceless lessons about the importance and value of work-life balance. They continue to bring me joy as they expand their own families. I cherish the presence in my life of my four siblings, Mark, Brent, Ross, and Alice, and their families. To Mark, who founded Kronos in 1977: you guided me expertly during our decades working together, always finding the right balance between the roles of company leader, boss, and brother. If anyone deserves credit for Kronos's success, it's you! I also wish to acknowledge my parents, Pearl and Jack Ain, whose example of love, altruism, and service to the community continues to inspire me. My thanks go out as well to my many friends, who make life so much fun. You know who you are!

Writing this book afforded me many blessings, but the greatest one was the chance to connect with Kronites in new and interesting ways. Building a strong culture requires constant care, vigilance, and hard work, but it becomes an inspired effort when you're surrounded by so many amazing people. To Kronites everywhere: *I genuinely care about each and every one of you.* Our company's success and the success of our customers owes to *you.* I always enjoy seeing and interacting with you at our offices around the world. You provide me with energy and a sense of purpose each and every day, and for that reason, I dedicate this book to you.

A NOTE ON SOURCES

This book draws on a research base of hundreds of documents, the vast majority of which came from inside our company. Sources consulted include:

INTERVIEWS

My research team and I interviewed dozens of current and former Kronites, some individually and others in small focus groups of 8 to 10 people. For added texture, we interviewed Kronos founder Mark Ain and other members of my family, as well as several current and former Kronos executives. We solicited further thoughts, insights, and data from interviewees and their teams via e-mails, and we also followed up with interviewees to fact-check stories as we represented them in the book. In a small number of cases, we performed interviews in written form via e-mail.

KRONOS REPORTS AND PRESENTATIONS

To collect Kronos data and insights, we drew upon a number of formal presentations and reports from various departments at Kronos, including marketing, human resources, finance, and so on.

KRONOS EMPLOYEE COMMUNICATIONS

We consulted hundreds of communications sent out by my executive team over the past decade, including our quarterly financial reports, my aron@work videos, personal e-mails from me and other executives to Kronites, our official Kronos cartoons, videos of presentations I've given at company events, and so on.

CONTEST SUBMISSIONS

As part of our research efforts, we consulted several of the lengthy submissions our corporate communications team prepares every year in order to be considered for external workplace honors and recognition.

SOCIAL MEDIA/E-MAIL

Our research team reviewed hundreds of Kronite postings on our internal collaboration site, as well as hundreds of e-mails I personally received and sent to Kronites around the world. We also collected comments from anonymous employees and former employees from LinkedIn, Glassdoor, and other external social media sites.

PUBLISHED/EXTERNAL SOURCES CONSULTED

Ain, Aron. "The CEO of Kronos on Launching an Unlimited Vacation Policy." *Harvard Business Review*, November/December 2017. https://hbr.org/2017/11/the-ceo-of-kronos-on-launching-an-unlimited-vacation-policy.

Business Wire. "Kronos Survey Reveals the Secrets to Day-to-Day Happiness in the Workplace: It's Easier (and Less Expensive) Than You Think." March 4, 2015. https://www.businesswire.com/news/home/20150304005465/en/Kronos-Survey-Reveals-Secrets-Day-to-day-Happiness-Workplace.

Huhman, Heather R. "Your Next 'Rockstar' Employee Might Be a Former One." *Entrepreneur*, February 5, 2018. https://www.entrepreneur.com/article/308368.

Indy Star. "Here It Is: The Text of Indiana's 'Religious Freedom' Law." April 2, 2015. https://www.indystar.com/story/news/politics/2015/03/27/text-indianas-religious-freedom-law/70539772/.

Kets de Vries, Manfred F. R. "Do You Hate Your Boss?" *Harvard Business Review*, December 2016. https://hbr.org/2016/12/do-you-hate-your-boss.

Lavelle, Lauren. "My Actress-Daughters Made the Touring Production of 'Annie,' But I Had a Full-Time Job." *Working Mother*, July 12, 2017. https://www.workingmother.com/interview-with-kristen-wylie.

Lombardi, Mollie. "Codename FALCON—Kronos Rethinks the Delivery of Workforce Management Solutions." *Aptitude Research Partners* (blog), November 13, 2017. http://www.aptituderesearchpartners.com/2017/11/13/codename-falcon-kronos-rethinks-the-delivery-of-workforce-management-solutions/.

Mueller, Holger. "Event Report—Kronos KronosWorks—Kronos Unleashes the Falcon—Launches Workforce Dimensions." *Enterprise Software Musings* (blog), December 3, 2017. https://enswmu.blogspot.com/2017/12/event-report-kronos-kronosworks-kronos.html?119efb1b=13295c78.

Reslen, Eileen. "The Perks at These Top Startups Will Make You Rethink Your 9-to-5." *Marie Claire*, November 1, 2017. https://www.marieclaire.com/career-advice/a13128496/linkedin-top-startups-companies-list-perks/.

Schawbel, Dan. "Candidates Are Now Competing Against Boomerang Employees for Jobs." *Forbes*, September 1, 2015. https://

www.forbes.com/sites/danschawbel/2015/09/01/candidates
-are-now-competing-against-boomerang-employees-for-jobs/
#71a795cb5c8b.

Schrodt, Paul. "12 Companies with the Most Luxurious Employee
Perks." *Time*, October 9, 2017. http://time.com/money/4972232/12
-companies-with-the-most-luxurious-employee-perks/.

Sinek, Simon. "Simon Sinek About Love, Relationships & Leadership."
YouTube, 12:42. September 18, 2017. https://www.youtube.com/wat
ch?v=dsQPhVwXcuc&feature=youtu.be.

Solomon, Lou. "The Top Complaints from Employees About Their Leaders." *Harvard Business Review*, June 24, 2015. https://hbr.org/2015
/06/the-top-complaints-from-employees-about-their-leaders.

UTEC. "Mission & Values." https://www.utec-lowell.org/about/mission
-values.

Workplace Trends. "The Corporate Culture and Boomerang Employee
Study." September 1, 2015. https://workplacetrends.com/the
-corporate-culture-and-boomerang-employee-study/.

Zillman, Claire. "Americans Are Still Terrible at Taking Vacations." *Fortune*, May 23, 2017. http://fortune.com/2017/05/23/vacation-time
-americans-unused/.

NOTES

INTRODUCTION

1. You can find the review at "Kronos Incorporated," *Glassdoor*, https://www.glassdoor.com/Reviews/Employee-Review-Kronos -Incorporated-RVW12720645.htm.

CHAPTER 2

1. *American Heritage® Dictionary of the English Language*, 5th ed. (Houghton Mifflin Harcourt, 2016), s.v. "kibitzer," accessed April 20, 2018, https://www.thefreedictionary.com/kibitzer.
2. "Kronos Incorporated," *Great Place to Work*, http://reviews .greatplacetowork.com/kronos-incorporated.

CHAPTER 3

1. "Kronos Incorporated," *Great Place to Work*, http://reviews .greatplacetowork.com/kronos-incorporated.

CHAPTER 4

1. Manfred F. R. Kets de Vries, "Do You Hate Your Boss?" *Harvard Business Review*, December 2016, https://hbr.org/2016/12/do-you-hate -your-boss.
2. Lou Solomon, "The Top Complaints from Employees About Their Leaders," *Harvard Business Review*, June 24, 2015, https://hbr .org/2015/06/the-top-complaints-from-employees-about-their -leaders.
3. "Making the 5HIFT: How Kronos Transformed from a Traditional Software Business into a SaaS Powerhouse," unpublished manuscript.

CHAPTER 6

1. Kronos press release, April 1, 2014.

CHAPTER 7

1. "Kronos Incorporated," *Great Place to Work*, http://reviews .greatplacetowork.com/kronos-incorporated.

CHAPTER 8

1. "Here It Is: The Text of Indiana's "Religious Freedom Law," *Indy Star*, updated April 2, 2015, https://www.indystar.com/story /news/politics/2015/03/27/text-indianas-religious-freedom-law /70539772/.

CHAPTER 9

1. Lauren Lavelle, "My Actress-Daughters Made the Touring Production of 'Annie,' But I Had a Full-Time Job," *Working Mother*, July 12, 2017, http://www.workingmother.com/interview-with-kristen -wylie.
2. "Kronos Incorporated," *Great Place to Work*, http://reviews .greatplacetowork.com/kronos-incorporated.
3. I tell the story of our adoption of myTime at length in "The CEO of Kronos on Launching an Unlimited Vacation Policy," *Harvard Business Review*, November-December 2017, https://hbr.org/2017/11/the -ceo-of-kronos-on-launching-an-unlimited-vacation-policy.
4. Claire Zillman, "Americans Are Still Terrible at Taking Vacations," *Fortune*, May 23, 2017, http://fortune.com/2017/05/23/vacation -time-americans-unused/.

CHAPTER 10

1. Heather R. Huhman, "Your Next 'Rockstar' Employee Might be a Former One," *Entrepreneur*, February 5, 2018, https:// www.entrepreneur.com/article/308368.
2. "The Corporate Culture and Boomerang Employee Study," *Workplace Trends*, September 1, 2015, https://workplacetrends.com/the -corporate-culture-and-boomerang-employee-study/.
3. Dan Schawbel, "Candidates Are Now Competing Against Boomerang Employees for Jobs," *Forbes*, September 1, 2015, https:// www.forbes.com/sites/danschawbel/2015/09/01/candidates -are-now-competing-against-boomerang-employees-for-jobs/ #71a795cb5c8b; Kerry Hannon, "Welcome Back: Boomerang Employees Are on the Rise," *Forbes*, September 7, 2015, https://www.forbes .com/sites/kerryhannon/2015/09/07/welcome-back-boomerang -employees-are-on-the-rise/#537591396eba; Joyce Maroney, "Organizations Warming Up to Boomerang Employees," *Huffington Post*, September 2, 2015, https://www.huffingtonpost.com/joyce-maroney /organizations-warming-up-_b_8071296.html.
4. "The Corporate Culture and Boomerang Employee Study," *Workplace Trends*, September 1, 2015, https://workplacetrends.com/the -corporate-culture-and-boomerang-employee-study/.
5. Ibid.

CHAPTER 11

1. "Kronos Survey Reveals the Secrets to Day-to-Day Happiness in the Workplace: It's Easier (and Less Expensive) Than You Think," *Business Wire*, March 4, 2015, https://www.businesswire.com/news /home/20150304005465/en/Kronos-Survey-Reveals-Secrets-Day -to-day-Happiness-Workplace.
2. "Making the 5HIFT: How Kronos Transformed from a Traditional Software Business into a SaaS Powerhouse," unpublished manuscript.

CHAPTER 12

1. "Kronos Incorporated," *Glassdoor*, https://www.glassdoor.com /Reviews/Employee-Review-Kronos-Incorporated-RVW16911836 .htm.

CHAPTER 13

1. Mollie Lombardi, "Codename FALCON—Kronos Rethinks the Delivery of Workforce Management Solutions," *Aptitude Research Partners*, November 13, 2017, http://www.aptituderesearchpartners .com/2017/11/13/codename-falcon-kronos-rethinks-the-delivery -of-workforce-management-solutions/.
2. Holger Mueller, "Event Report—Kronos KronosWorks—Kronos Unleashes the Falcon—Launches Workforce Dimensions," *Enterprise Software Musings*, https://enswmu.blogspot.com/2017 /12/event-report-kronos-kronosworks-kronos.html?119efb1b= 13295c78.
3. Quoted in *Making the 5HIFT: How Kronos Transformed from a Traditional Software Business into a SaaS Powerhouse,* unpublished booklet manuscript.

CHAPTER 14

1. "Mission & Values," UTEC, https://www.utec-lowell.org/about /mission-values.

EPILOGUE

1. This quote is adapted from Simon Sinek's speech about Love, Relationships & Leadership, YouTube, September 18, 2017, https://www .youtube.com/watch?v=dsQPhVwXcuc&feature=youtu.be.

INDEX

ABOUT THE AUTHOR

Aron **Ain** is chief executive officer of Kronos Incorporated, a global provider of workforce management and human capital management cloud solutions. Since joining the company in 1979, Ain has played a role in nearly every functional department, helping to build what is today a $1.4 billion global enterprise software powerhouse.

Ain has helped revolutionize how organizations manage their workforces with a new generation of products and services that empower employees to work smarter, work their way, and work in a modern cloud. Under his leadership, Kronos's employee engagement scores have risen to record heights, and the organization has received numerous awards for its culture and employee experience for multiple years running. Great Place to Work has certified Kronos as a top workplace; Glassdoor honored Kronos with its Employees' Choice award, recognizing the 100 Best Places to Work; and *Fortune* magazine named Kronos one of its 100 Best Companies to Work For.

Media around the world have covered Ain and his commitment to employee engagement and inspired leadership, including *Harvard Business Review*, *New York Times*, and NPR. Ain has also won numerous prestigious awards, including the Massachusetts High Technology Council's Ray Stata Leadership and Innovation Award, the Mass Technology Leadership Council's CEO of the Year award, and Ernst & Young's Entrepreneur of the Year award. Glassdoor has repeatedly named him to its list of highest-rated CEOs in the United States, a recognition based entirely on employee reviews.

Ain serves on the Board of Trustees of his alma mater, Hamilton College, and offers his leadership advice and experience to numerous organizations in various volunteer roles. He takes great satisfaction in serving his community and helping others live more productive and meaningful lives.

Ain received his bachelor's degree in economics and government from Hamilton. He has also participated in a series of executive education programs, including the AEA/Stanford Executive Institute at Stanford University.